D0897757

The Orkney Dictionary

Margaret Flaws
Gregor Lamb

Orkney Language and Culture Group

© Margaret Flaws, Gregor Lamb, 1996

First printed 1996

Second edition 2001

Typesetting by Dod Flaws, Dr John Sinclair

Printed by The Orcadian Limited, Kirkwall, Orkney

Published by The Orkney Language and Culture Group

ISBN 0 9529324 1 5

The Orkney Dictionary

Foreword

Throughout the twentieth century it has been observed that the Orcadian dialect is in decline. The reasons for this are several and interconnected – the increased mobility of people to and from the islands, and importantly within them, the tendency towards centralisation and the all-pervasiveness of the media, nationally and internationally – all of these factors have tended to promote standardisation and the suppression of individuality. In Orkney our uniqueness is exemplified by our dialect. Unfortunately standard English has become locally the preferred form of the written and spoken word.

So how to halt the decline, and even reverse the trend? In 1992, an Orkney Language and Culture Group was formed, with a membership of people all with a high profile in the field of education. Their stated aim was to promote and develop all aspects of Orcadian language and culture in schools, in particular, the Orcadian dialect which reflects the history of the community and is an integral part of the language children bring to school.

To encourage contemporary usage of Orcadian dialect in poetry, prose and speech, a vocabulary must form the basis. Schools suggested that an easily accessible reference book would help.

Two established authors on dialect matters were approached – Margaret Flaws and Gregor Lamb – and the Group, under the chairmanship of Harvey Johnston, undertook the compilation of a dialect dictionary to be aimed at Orkney's school pupils. As the scope of the project widened, the Group came to see "The Orkney Dictionary" as more than just a school reference, but a volume for day to day use by all ages.

In the approach to the twenty-first century, the Orkney Language and Culture Group earnestly hope it has contributed in some small way to the preservation of our unique cultural heritage.

Ian Murdo MacDonald
Chair, Education Committee
Orkney Islands Council
(1994 – 1999)

A Word for the Bairns

Oh bairns be prood to use the words
That in this book you'll find
Mak sure they're often on yer lips
And always in yer mind

And then wan day you'll realise
When you are no so young
That Orkney's greatest treasure is
By far its mither tongue

Harvey Johnston

Acknowledgements

We should like to take this opportunity to thank the Education Department of Orkney Islands Council for the bold and imaginative steps they have taken to foster the island dialect and it is in this spirit that The Orkney Dictionary is born. The authors, Margaret Flaws and Gregor Lamb are delighted to have been associated with this work and we should like to thank personally those who had faith in us to bring this work to fruition. Is should be stressed however that the authors do not take all the credit for this production. Unlike most authors we were fortunate to have the assistance of a back-up team of Orkney dialect enthusiasts who fed in much useful material, who undertook proof reading, who made suggestions of production, design and format and whose work in these fields was greatly valued. They are:-

The publishers, the Orkney Language and Culture Group.

Members: Harvey Johnston, Chair
Belle Drever, Administration
Karen Esson
Bertha Fiddler
Bobby Leslie
Ian MacDonald
W. Leslie Manson
Bryce Wilson
Jocky Wood

Other Contributors and Proof Readers.

Peggy Costie, Westray
Dave and Daisy Craigie, Wyre and Burray
Rolf Heggnes, Fana, Norway
Sam Harcus, Westray
Thora Mary Linklater, Stenness
Nancy Scott, Westray
Beatrice Thomson, North Ronaldsay

Secretarial Support:
    Elaine Dunne, Kirkwall

Printers: *The Orcadian*, and in particular Stewart Davidson for contributions and advice.

Typesetters: Dod Flaws
                Dr John Sinclair

Cover   Shona Thomson

ooooooooooooooooooooooo

The Orkney Language and Culture Group would like to thank the following for financial assistance:-

Elf Consortium
Orkney Vintage Club
The Orkney Educational Trust
The Community Councils of: Birsay; Eday; Evie and Rendall; Firth and Sunnybrae; Flotta; Graemsay, Hoy and Walls; Harray and Stenness; Kirkwall and St Ola; Papa Westray; Rousay, Egilsay and Wyre; St Andrews; Sanday; Sandwick; South Ronaldsay and Burray; Stronsay;

Historical Perspective

In Orkney today we speak a dialect of Scots but we have an accent which is all our own and we also have many words which people from the Mainland of Scotland would not recognise. The words we use and they way we use them are very similar to words and phrases in the Shetland dialect but they are not exactly alike, so we cannot call our dialect 'Northern Islands Scots'. In fact if we are asked what language we speak, we say Orcadian. To understand how we came to speak this particular language, we must look at the history of Orkney.

The first people who lived in Orkney left behind many stone buildings and later some carved stones, but we do not know what language they spoke. It would have been a Pictish language, but even that does not help us much as no-one knows what language the Picts used. It might have been some form of Celtic (Gaelic) but it could have been something completely different. The only thing we know for certain is that their language disappeared when the Norse settlers came to Orkney.

The Norsemen brought their own language with them and for many centuries Norse was spoken throughout Orkney and Shetland. This was the language used in Norway, Sweden, Denmark, Iceland, the Faeroes and Orkney and Shetland. When Orkney and Shetland were originally taken over by the Norsemen, the language used was the same over all these countries but gradually through the centuries each country developed its own form. In Orkney and Shetland our form became known as the Norn. Today, Norse has split up into Icelandic, Faeroese, Norwegian, Swedish and Danish and the Norn has almost disappeared - almost, but not completely as we shall see.

In 1468 Orkney was handed over to Scotland, followed by Shetland in 1469, and after that any records that were kept were written in Scots. Scots became the official language and was used for any legal documents and for trade. The Norn was still used at home of course among the greater part of the people in Orkney, but to deal with the officials sent from Scotland to govern Orkney and to trade with Scotland, people would have had to learn to speak Scots. It is thus not surprising that the Norn began to disappear and that Scots gradually replaced it everywhere. The Norn would have disappeared from the towns of Kirkwall and Stromness first until eventually it would have been spoken only in country districts and the Isles.

We can almost set an exact date for the end of the Norn: 1750. At this date we find the last references to it on the Mainland of Orkney. Perhaps it was a slightly later date in the further North Isles, as we find a reference in

I

Historical Perspective

Barry's History of Orkney to Norse ballads being sung in North Ronaldsay. Although we have these references to the Norn, we cannot tell exactly how it was spoken at that time as there are no written records. There are a few clues, however, as one or two people took the trouble to write down a little of it, but as they were not Norn speakers themselves we cannot rely on their spelling. Here is the Lord's Prayer from Orkney which was written down at this time:

Favor i er i chimeri
 Helleut ir i nam thite, gilla cosdum thite cumma,
 Veya thine mota vara gort o yurn sinna gort i chimeri,
 Ga vus da on da dalight brow vora,
 Firgive vus sinna vora sin vee firgive sindara mutha vus
 Lyv vus ye i tumtation,
 Men delivra vus fro olt ilt, Amen.

At first sight this seems like a foreign language indeed, but if you look at it more closely and compare it with the Lord's Prayer (in English) with which we are familiar it is possible to recognise many of the words. More can be recognised if we change *v* into *w* at the beginning of words. For example, in line 5, *vee firgive* becomes *we forgive*. Still more can be recognised if we forget about English and use Orcadian. In line 1, *er* is how we say English *are*. In line 4, *ga* becomes *gae*, which we use for English *give*.

The words are easy to understand. What is strange is the order of the words. Instead of *'forgive is wir sins'*, we have *'firgive vus sinna vora'*. There is a clue here to the reason the Norn disappeared, if indeed it did disappear. If we can recognise the words but not the syntax, that is the order in which they are used, this ought to mean that the words used in the Lord's Prayer as it is written above are Scots but the syntax is the Norn. This, however, is not so: the words are Norn also. A large number of the words used in Scots were used also in Norse as those languages were alike in many ways, and so, when Orcadians had to learn Scots, they would have found that they knew a great deal of it already and had only to change the syntax around to make themselves understood readily.

Because Orkney is so close to Scotland, some Orcadians would have been familiar with Scots long before 1468 and without doubt many people from the Mainland of Scotland would have settled in Orkney throughout the centuries bringing their language with them. With all of this contact it would

II

seem likely that Scots would have had an influence on the Norn even if Orkney had not been handed over to Scotland.

As the words used in Scots and the Norn are so alike, it is impossible for us to tell, a lot of the time, if we are using a Scots word or a Norn word. It is a shared inheritance. We do have a lot of words and phrases, though, which are not used in Scots and we have hung on to them because they were useful, because they were words to do with everyday tasks in farming and fishing, or words for birds and flowers, or phrases which had no equivalent in Scots.

If Scots had been a completely different language to the Norn and none of the words had been the same, we would have lost most, if not all, of the Norn. This is what happened in many areas of Scotland which used to speak Gaelic. There is no mixture of Gaelic and Scots, but there is quite definitely a mixture of Scots and the Norn.

Over the last hundred years however there have been other changes to our language. English replaced Scots as the official language, the language to use in records and legal documents. Teachers insisted on English as 'correct speech' in schools:
Don't say 'noo', say 'now',
Don't say 'ku', say 'cow'.
C.M.Costie, 'Speech'.

Over the last hundred years also we have lost a great number of the words we once used. If we look at Dr. Hugh Marwick's Orkney Norn, written 70 years ago, we can see this. Our language is still changing too. As we listen to the radio and watch television, we are influenced by English speakers, American, even Australian. The number of people speaking Orcadian on the radio or television is very small, especially since most Orcadians use English if they are broadcasting.

There is no doubt that we have lost a great deal of the Norn. We should not be surprised at this when we consider the facts that teachers once insisted on English and that we hear such different language on radio and television. The surprise lies in the fact that so much of it still exists. The Norn, and Orcadian, must be a very strong plant to have survived as it has done all these centuries and now, at the end of the twentieth century, we still have a language of our own, Orcadian. We have access to all the riches of the English language with a richness of our own to fall back on when English fails us. We are indeed fortunate.

Pronunciation

This dictionary lists dialect words which are not normally found in an English dictionary. It also includes English words and phrases which are used in Orkney in a special way. However the reader will also find in the lists English words which are spelt differently. This is to help the reader to pronounce the word and to write and recognise it in Orcadian. For a number of reasons it has not been possible to include every word which is pronounced differently. Firstly, so many English words are changed when pronounced by an Orcadian that if we had included them all we would have ended up with a heavy and costly book. Secondly it is very difficult to write some of our pronunciations because there is no English vowel which we can use to represent the sound. Take the word 'fish' for example. As an Orcadian you may think that you pronounce this in an 'English' fashion but you do not. Say 'fish', then ask an English speaker to say the same word and note the difference. There is no way in which this difference can be written so you will not find 'fish' in the dictionary! When you are having this little game why not say 'Birsay' - in Orcadian of course - and ask the English speaker to repeat exactly what you say. You will find that the English speaker is unable to copy you! Just as it is not possible to write 'fish' in the way that Orcadians pronounce it, it is not possible to write 'Birsay' either unless we add new letters to the alphabet!

Orcadians in their speech use a number of sounds which are unknown in English but which are used for example in Norwegian and the Norwegians have special letters for these sounds. Take for example the Orkney word for a coalfish - a *cuithe*. The sound in the middle can easily be written in Norwegian with the special letter ø. When the committee who planned this dictionary was discussing how the Orkney words should be written, there was a great debate about whether letter ø should be used to represent this sound or whether in fact we should do as the Shetlanders do since they have the same problem. They chose the German and Icelandic letter ö. In the end the committee decided to use English letters wherever possible so you will find that in this dictionary the vowels **ui** or sometimes **eu** together are used to represent this sound and so a *cuithe* remains a *cuithe*.

The non-Orcadian reader will be interested to know whether there are any pronunciation rules. When advising on pronunciation, dictionary makers have to be very careful since just as the pronunciation of English varies greatly from one part of Britain to the other, so the pronunciation of Orcadian varies from parish to parish and from island to island. Perhaps the greatest difference lies in the pronunciation of words in the north Isles and on The Mainland. Words ending in 'ead' such as **head, dead** and **bread** are sounded 'heid', 'deid' and 'breid'. There is evidence that this is a relic of a pronunciation which at one time was found throughout Orkney since the word **dread** is pronounced 'dreed' everywhere. Several other North Isles words change in the same way. **Name** is pronounced 'neem' and **tale**, sounded 'teel', whereas **table** is 'teeble' and **able** 'eeble'. North Ronaldsay folk pronounce the long **i** as 'oi'; in this way **mile** is sounded 'moile' and **while** as 'whoile'. Like Westray folk they also pronounce the short **a** as 'ay' in which case **apple** becomes 'ayple' and **barn** 'bayrn'. Where an **a** is followed by an 'r' the position is complicated. On The Mainland, west of the range of hills which passes through Birsay and Harray, an **a** followed by a **r** is sounded as if it were a short 'e'. In this way **car** becomes 'ker', **guitar**, 'guit-er'. North Isles folk might say 'Er thoo?' instead of 'Are thoo?' When **ar** is followed by **t** as in **part, smart, cart, start**, such words are universally pronounced as 'pert', 'smert', 'kert' and 'stert' but there is no rule for other 'art' type words; 'mart' and 'wart' for example are regular. As for the word **arm** it is regularly pronounced 'erm' throughout Orkney.

We also have to remember that, as in any dialect, pronunciation is changing rapidly and there are great differences between one generation and another. For instance in the examples below, the **oo** sound in English which is pronounced 'ui' in dialect does not seem to have been adopted by the younger generation, few of whom would talk about the *muin* for the 'moon' or *skuil* for 'school'.

The following guidelines therefore are general and are certainly not intended to indicate that any one pronunciation is superior to another.

Consonants

The sound of some consonants differ from English. A hard **c** or **k** may still be heard pronounced 'ch' in the North Isles, especially in North Ronaldsay. e.g. **care** becomes 'chair', **cake** 'chek', **kiosk** 'chosk'. One

V

might joke that when one North Ronaldsay chicken meets another it enquires, 'Hoo are thoo cheepan?' This pronunciation does not exist on The Mainland though we know it did exist and can be seen in placenames such as the Chair o the Lyde where 'chair' is the same word as Norwegian dialect *kjerr* a bog. Some old folks pronounce *k* as a *t*. If they do so they generally introduce a *y* immediately after it so that **kettle** becomes *tyettle*. The consonant **d** is often lost if it appears in conjunction with **l**, e.g **candle** becomes 'canle' and **handle**, hanle. As in English dialect **old** loses its final **d** to becomes 'aal' and **cold** is rendered 'caal'. Both **j** and soft **g** are usually pronounced 'ch' throughout Orkney and so **German jam** becomes 'Cherman cham'. The policy adopted in the compilation of the dictionary is not to reject the 'ch' spelling of words beginning with **j** and soft **g** and we should like to recommend that dialect writers also adopt this approach. **H** is always sounded at the beginning of a word, the main exception being the word **hospital**, always pronounced 'ospital'. **House** also loses its initial **h** in the common expression *wir oos*, 'our house'. Many older people still pronounce **qu** as 'wh'. An instruction to a child to stop doing something was, 'White hid!' which means 'Quit that!' **S** is pronounced as in English unless there is an **r** sound in front of it in which case, in some parts of Orkney but excluding the North Isles, the **s** is pronounced 'sh'. English **worse** for example is pronounced 'warsh'. Even where a word ending with an **r** sound is followed by a word beginning with an **s**, this **s** will also be changed to 'sh'. **More supper** becomes therefore in, chiefly Mainland, dialect 'more shupper'. **Th** at the beginning and end of words always used to be pronounced as **t**. **Length** would be 'lent', **earth** 'ert' and the parish of **Firth**, 'Firt'. **Thing** would be sounded 'ting' and **think** as 'tink'. Such pronunciations may still be heard though 'doo' and 'dee', the old dialect pronunciation of 'thoo' and 'thee' is completely lost. **Wh** in initial position is always sounded, unlike in English. For example whereas **wheel** in English is sounded 'weel' Orcadians would sound the complete word. Initial **z** is pronounced 's', hence **zoo** and **zebra** become 'soo' and 'sebra'.

Vowels

The letter **l** in a word frequently affects the sound of the vowel in front of it. Where **a** is followed by a double 'l' the **a** becomes short. **All** becomes 'aal', **tall** becomes 'taal' and **wall** becomes 'waal' (or shorter 'wa') and so on. Where a short **e** is follwed by a double **l** the **e** is sounded 'ay', for example **sell**, **yell** and **hell** are rendered 'sayl', 'yayl' and 'hayl'. There are important exceptions to this as in the case of **well** (in the sense of 'healthy') which is pronounced 'weel' and **well** meaning a spring of water which on The Mainland is pronounced 'waal'[1]. Where **e** is followed by 'w' as in **new** or **few** the **e** is sounded approximately 'ow' on The Mainland. An Orcadian seeing a neighbour might enquire 'Whit nows wi thee the day?' meaning 'What news with you today?' The dialect pronunciation in the North Isles of **e** followed by 'w' has no equivalent English dipthong. Where a long **i** is followed by 'nd' the tendency is for the **i** to be short as in 'blind', 'find', 'wind' (round), 'grind' all of which rhyme with 'wind' in the sense of 'gale'. Important exceptions are 'mind' and 'kind' which are sounded as in English. The short 'i' is usually pronounced as in English but there are several important exceptions in which it is pronounced 'ee'. For example **wicked**, **king**, **kick**, **basin** and **kitchen** are pronounced 'weekid', 'keeng', 'besseen' and 'keetcheen'. The short **i** in the gerund ending as for example in English **fishing** is also sounded 'ee' and since the 'g' sound of the gerund is always dropped the reader will find in the dictionary that all gerunds are written in the form 'fisheen', 'wirkeen' and so on. This applies to other nouns which have the 'ing' suffix, e.g. 'pudding', which appears here as 'puddeen' which happens to have a short 'u' in Orcadian to make things even more complicated! The English long **o** as in **rope**, **broke** and **soap** for example is pronounced as a short **o** in Orcadian and become therefore 'rop', 'brok' and 'sop'. The old pronuciation of the short **o** was 'ae' so **rope** was 'raep' and **soap**, 'saep'. It is still possible to hear **soap** pronounced in this way though the pronunciation 'raep' is reserved only for the line or rod (originally **rope**) above a fireplace. In instances where the long **o** is followed by l the sound of the **o** is changed to 'ow' and so **old** becomes 'owld', **cold** 'cowld' and so on. English words ending in -**ull** have two different pronunciations, for example **full** and **dull**. In Orcadian all words ending in -**ull** are pronounced as English **dull**.

Diphthongs

English	Orcadian	Examples of Orcadian	Examples of exceptions
ea	ae (see note above on North Isles pronunciation of 'ead' type words)	'peat' becomes *paet*	leap (*leep*), leave (*layve*), great (*gret*), leak (*lek*), steal (*stale*), dream (*draym*)
ou, ow	oo	'sound' becomes *soond* 'pour' becomes *poor* 'now' becomes *noo* 'bow' (of a boat) becomes *boo* 'towel' becomes *tooel*	ground (*grund*), low, mound, £-pound (all pronounced as in English)
oa	o	'boat' becomes *bot*	
ay	ey	'away' becomes *awey* 'hay' becomes *hey*	say, lay, day, play are pronounced as in English
oo	ui/eu	'moon' becomes *muin* 'soon' becomes *suin* 'fool' becomes *fuil* 'to' and 'do' (which have an 'oo' sound in English) become *teu* and *deu*	
au, aw	aa[1]	'haul' becomes *haal* 'fault' becomes *faalt* 'law' becomes *laa* 'saw' becomes *saa* 'shawl' becomes *shaal*	
ai	ey	'hail' becomes *hel* sounded as in English 'hel(p)' 'nail' becomes *nel*	pail is sounded as in English

[1] no English vowel or diphthong can represent the sound of the 'aa' in Orcadian 'waal' meaning a spring of water. Though 'waal' is used to mean spring of water and wall in this dictionary their pronunciation is completely different. The Rousay, Evie and Rendall pronunciation of 'aal' meaning **all** contains the same vowel as 'waal' meaning a spring of water.

Grammar

This dictionary gives a list of words which are used in Orcadian and which might not be found in other dialects. However it is not only the words in Orcadian which are different but the way and the order in which we use them also, so this book would be incomplete without a short description of the grammar of Orcadian, in so far as it is different from English.

Some of the differences are as follows:

ARTICLES:
The definite article is 'the'. As in Scots it is used with a number of nouns with which it would not be used in English. For example, *gaan tae the kirk/the skuil; gotten the maesles; makkan the dinner.* In North Ronaldsay it is pronounced like '*they*'.

The indefinite article is always 'a', never 'an'.

NOUNS:
The plural form of nouns is, as in English, formed by adding 's', but there are some exceptions to this. Some of these are listed, as for example 'horse'. Units of measurement often have the same form for both singular and plural, for example *three pund o sugar, twa unce o bakki.*

PRONOUNS:
Personal pronouns. The second person singular pronoun '*thoo*' is still used when addressing a friend, a family member or someone younger. *Thoo* is used with a verb form, in the present tense, ending in 's':
   Whit dis thoo think o that?
   Tak thee book wi thee when thoo goes tae bed.

Demonstrative pronouns are this and that for both singular and plural. *This eens is better as that eens.*

Relative pronoun is '*at*' instead of 'who', 'which' or 'that'. *That's the man at cam tae the door.*

Whitna/whitan can be used interrogatively or demonstratively.
Whitna man's that?
Whitan kye is yin in the aets?

For whitna grand frock!
Whitan bonnie flooers!
As a general rule, *whitna* is used in the singular and *whitan* in the plural.

VERBS.
The verb '**to be**':

Present tense.	**Ah'm**	I'm	**Wir**	We're
	Thoo're	You're	**Yir**	You're
	He's	He's	**Thir**	They're

The verb '**to be**' is used as an auxiliary instead of English 'to have', for example;
Ah'm meed the dinner: I have made dinner.
Wir biggid the stack: We have built the stack..
Thoo'll be gotten a fair price for thee kye: You will have got a good price for your cattle.
Hid'll lickly be been shoved in a draaer somewey: It will likely have been put into a drawer somewhere.

Subjunctive tense of verb '**to be**' is '**bees**'.
Thoo'll git a sweetie if thoo bees good.
We'll can stert cuttan the morn if hid bees dry.
Note that the verb '**can**' is often used in Orcadian to express English '**be able to**'.

Thir is used also for 'there is', 'there are'.
Thir a coo lowse in the byre.
Thir a lok o fock here.

They wir is also used for 'there was', 'there were'.
They wir a coo lowse in the byre.
They wir a lok o fock there.

X

Verbal adjective/present participle. In Orcadian this ends in '**-an**'.
Whit's thee mither deuan? Sheu's knittan.
Whit's thee fether deuan? He's plooan.

Verbal noun. In Orcadian this ends in '**-een**'.
Whit's thee mither deuan? Sheu's deuan her knitteen.
Whit's thee fether deuan? He's at the plooeen.
This form of the verb is also used as a noun qualifier with another noun.
knitteen-needles; plooeen-match.

These two forms, of the verbal adjective and noun, are distinct, are used automatically and are never confused.

Past tense and past participle.
As in English, these can be formed by adding '-ed'. However a number of verbs which take '-ed' in English have '-id' in Orcadian, for example jumped, *jumpid;* looked, *lukkid.* Other examples will be found in this dictionary, together with the verbs which have different past tenses in Orcadian.

XI

Spelling

Until recently, it was possible to tell exactly which island or part of the Mainland anyone came from by the way they spoke. It is still possible to some extent but not with the same amount of accuracy. This means that, although we speak of Orcadian as a single dialect, within that dialect there are many different ways of saying the same word; and this in turn makes compiling a dictionary of Orcadian quite difficult.

The problem can be solved in two different ways. One way is to pick one pronunciation of a word and decide that that should be the standard form, but this would mean losing a lot of the variety, colour and interest of the dialect. The second method is to include as many different pronunciations as possible to show the variations between districts, and this is the method we have chosen.

Until now there has been no guide to help with spelling Orcadian and this has meant a wide variety in spelling which makes it difficult for the reader. We have therefore tried to bring order and consistency into the spelling of Orcadian sounds. As far as possible we have followed English spelling conventions as these are the most familiar. We learn them in our first year at school. If an English word is used in Orcadian with only a slight difference in pronunciation, we see no reason to change it. For example, although we pronounce the letter 'j' in Orcadian as 'ch', we see no reason to drop the letter 'j' in spelling. Orcadians always pronounce 'j' as 'ch' when reading English and will therefore have no trouble in doing the same when reading Orcadian. In fact, to change the spelling to 'ch' each time makes Orcadian more difficult to read as we are used to the convention of spelling with 'j'.

As far as possible we have used familiar spellings and we hope that our approach is one of common sense. We have added the following conventions to help with the spelling of Orcadian words:

AA is used to represent the long 'a' sound in *gaan* (going) as opposed to *gan* (stare).

AE is used for the sound in Orcadian *paet, maet* etc. (English peat, meat.)

EI is used as in Scots to show the dialect equivalent of a word which would have EA in English, for example *heid, breid* for head, bread.

EY is used, not as in English grey, but as a diphthong which English does not have. Examples: *wey,* (way), *gey,* (quite).

UI and **EU** are used for the sound in, for example, *cuithe,* which is similar to French 'eu'. A general rule is followed whereby **UI** is used at the beginning and in the middle of words, and **EU** is reserved for endings, for example *sheu.*

Y is used in the middle of words to represent the sound in 'why'. The exception to this is when it follows 'g', as in *gyung,* when it should be pronounced as in 'young'.

AU is used only to illustrate the North Ronaldsay pronunciation of **a + n** as in *aund,* and. It should be pronounced as in English 'fault'.

Use of the apostrophe:
There is a tendency, when writing dialect, to put in an apostrophe whenever it is considered that a letter is missing from the English equivalent of a word. For example, many writers put in an apostrophe after o' (thus), meaning English "of". We consider that there is no need to do this since it is dialect which is being written, and in Orcadian we use the word "o", not the word "of". Similarly there is no need to put in an apostrophe after the present participle, indicating a missing **g**, as the present participle in Orcadian ends in **-an**. An apostrophe should be used only to indicate that a letter is missing in Orcadian, as for example "**Ah'm**" for "I am".

To show the diversity of pronunciation within Orkney we have tried to use examples of speech from as many places as possible, but we have not specified in the main body of text which areas these examples come from. While examples from North Ronaldsay are readily identifiable by the use of soft 'j' for hard 'g' among other features, we believe that readers will be able to deduce the origins of the others fairly easily. We hope, in this way, that we have managed to show a little of the variety and richness of our dialect.

How to use this dictionary

If you cannot find the word you are looking for, try a different spelling; for example look for *clatter* under *klatter.*

If you still have difficulty finding the word, check that it is not in an English or a Scots dictionary. This Orcadian dictionary is designed to be used in conjunction with a Scots dictionary and therefore does not include many common Scots words.

The English into Orcadian section should be used as a reference only, and the words given there should be looked up in the Orcadian into English section for examples of usage.

For further study of Orcadian and an extended word list, the following books should be consulted: *Orkney Wordbook*:   Gregor Lamb.
                                                 The Orkney Norn: Dr. Hugh Marwick.

Abreviations

n.	noun
v.	verb
p.t.	past tense.
p.p.	past participle.
adj.	adjective.
adv.	adverb.
prep.	preposition
conj.	conjunction
exclam.	exclamation.
pron.	pronoun.
†	archaic word or object.

A

a *ind. art.* generally always used before vowels. *tae boil a egg.*

a-back *adv.* (always used negatively) backward, shy, *'He's no a-back o askan.'*

a-paece *adv.* still, in peace. *'Sit a-paece beuy!.'*

aa, aal *adj.* all.

aabody *n.* everybody.

aafil, aafu *adj.* awful: also used as *adv.*

aak[1] *v.* be about to be sick or to cough up phlegm. *akkan and spittan* spitting.

aak[2] *n.* 1 the common guillemot. 2 nickname for Westray people.

aan *n.* awn (barley).

aboot *prep.* about. **aboot ages** about the same age, *'He wis aboot ages wi me.'* **aboot-gaan buddy, gaan-aboot buddy** a person who always seems to be visiting or going about. **aboot-hands (wi)** in the vicinity, *'Is thee mither aboot-hands?'* **home-aboot** in or around the house, *'He lay home-aboot for a while.'* **in-aboot** inside, *'Bide in-aboot, bairns, till that unkan man's by.'* **oot-aboot** out and about, *'Willie can get oot-aboot noo the weather's warmer.'* **aboot-kast** a sudden change in the direction of the wind. **aboot-gaan** variable, *'Hid's a aboot-gaan wind.'*

abuin, abune *prep.* above.

accorned, accorn, accorun *adv.* according, *'Ah'll gae yi accorned tae whit I hiv.'* **accorned tae the man** as it is said. *'Ah'll gae thee sometheen tae weet thee trapple accorned tae the man.'*

Adam *n.* the dark purple orchid.

aest *n.* east. *'A wind fae the aest is no good tae man or baest.'*

aet *v.* eat. *'Hid'll aet afore a stone.'* It is better than no food at all.

aets *n.* oats.

aff *adv.* off. *'Ah'm aff the mind o hid.'* I've changed my mind. **aff-casteens** *n.* second-hand belongings. **aff-faas** *n.* the left-overs. **aff-pit, pit-aff** *n.* delay. **afftak** *n.* a lull in a storm. **aff-takkan** *adj.* ridiculing, sarcastic. *'He his a kinda aff-takkan wey wi him.'* **aff the baet** unwell.

affens *adv.* often.

aff-lay *n.* fluency, fluent speech, *'He wid mak a grand cooncillor. He his a right aff-lay.'*

affrontid *adj.* ashamed. *'I wis just black affrontid when the mineester cam in and the hoose in sic a steer.'*

afore *prep.* 1 before. 2 over, *tae go afore the craig* to take one's life by jumping over a cliff; *pittan bruck afore the shore* tipping rubbish on the shore. **afore a face** *adv.* headlong, pell-mell.

1

agee *adj.* (of a door etc.) squint.

aggle, haggle *v.* to make a mess. *n.* a mess.

Ah *first person singular* I, in present tense of verb 'to be', in future and perfect tenses e.g. *'Ah'm right playsed tae see thee.'* *'Ah'll see thee the morn.'* *'Ah'm been tae Hoy afore.'*

ahint *prep.* behind.

aicher *n.* ear of corn or barley.

aikaspire, aikelspeckled *adj.* mouldy.

ain, own *adj.* own, *'Luk efter thee ain bairns.'*

air, aer *v.* taste. *n.* 1 air. 2 a small quantity, *'Pit a aer o tea in the pot.'*

aire, ayre *n.* a gravelly point usually enclosing a small lagoon.

airt, aert *n.* a direction, *'The lum'll no draa whin the wind's in this airt.'*

aisins *n.* the eaves of a house.

aithken, euchen *n.* a mark on a sheep to denote ownership.

aize *v.* 1 ease. 2 blaze. **aizer, eezer** *n.* a roaring fire. **aizement** *n.* relief.

alamotti *n.* the stormy petrel.

alat *adv.* wrong, not the usual.

alwis *adv.* always.

ammers *n.* embers.

amis, amas *adj.* 1 wretched, *amis ting o bairn* sickly child 2 deserved, *'I thowt hid wis amis on him when he fell aff the bike efter hittan her.'* *'Hid wud be amas tae gae yin cat a bit o maet.'* **Amis on thee!** Serves you right.

andoo *v.* 1 row a boat against wind or tide so that it keeps in position for fishing etc. 2 stroll.

ane, een, wan *num.* one.

animal *n.* animal. **animals** cattle, *'Me son only works wi sheep, he disna hiv any animals.'*

annoyed *adj.* 1 annoyed. 2 worried.

answer *v.* obey, *'That thing o bairn'll no answer.'*

anteran *adj.* odd in the sense of occasional. *'Hid's December noo and we just git a anteran egg fae the hens.'*

anywey, onywey *adv.* anyhow.

ap *prep.* up. **ap the spoot** offended.

apae, apin *prep.* upon.

arboo *n.* maggots in an animal's back.

arby *n.* the sea pink.

ark *n.* something large. *a great ark o a hoose.*

arkmae *n.* large heavy article, also used of seals etc. *'Yin's a arkmae o a fish.'*

arroo *n.* a pullet. *arroo eggs* pullet eggs.

arvo, ervo *n.* chickweed.

as *prep.* 1 as. 2 than, *better as his.*

ashet *n.* large serving plate.

aside *prep.* beside.

ass *n.* ash. **assie pattle** *n.* 1 a lazy person who stays at home and pokes in the ashes. 2 a nickname for someone from Sandwick, Orkney.

asticle *n.* glazing bar in windows.

at[1] *conj.* that, *'I tellt him at I couldna come.'*

at² *prep.* at, *'Whar are we at noo?'* Where are we?

atfers *n.* manner, appearance, behaviour. *'I didno like his atfers.'* I did not like the look of him.

atgyong, atjaan *n.* approach, competence, *'Sheu haed nee atgyong.'*

atlukkan *adj.* inquisitive.

at-pitten, pitten-at *adj.* annoyed.

atween, awheen *prep.* between. *a day atween weathers* a mild day between stormy days.

auld, aald, owld *adj.* old. **Auld Nick** the devil. **auld farrant** old fashioned **Auld New Year's Day** 13th January. **Auld Hallowmas** 1st November.

aumrie, amerie *n.* a cupboard, generally built with stone.

ava *adv.* at all, *'There wis nobody there ava.'*

awa, awey *adv.* away.

axe, exe *n.* **1** axe. **2** a North Ronaldsay sheep mark.

aye, ey *exclam.* **1** yes. *'Aye wid he.'* He certainly would. **2** Hello! in a greeting but more generally **aye aye.** *adv.* always, *'He's aye gaan there.'*

B

ba *n.* ball. **The Ba** the traditional ball games held in Kirkwall on Christmas Day and New Year's Day. **ba o the leg** the calf of the leg.

baakie *n.* great black-backed gull.

back, bawk *n.* **1** crossbeam (usually **couple-backs** or **twart-backs**). **2** a hens' roost.

back *n.* back. **at the back o** after, *at the back o dinner time, at the back o twal.* **back and fore** to and fro. **back-brakkan** *adj.* (of work) hard. **back-comeen** *n.* retribution, comeback, *'Better dae the job right so thir's no backcomeen.'* **back-door trot/gallop** diarrhoea. **backend** *the backend o the year* harvest time. **backleens, backlins** *adv.* backwards. **backside** *n.* the rump. **backside foremost** back to front (of a jersey, cap etc). **back-speir** *v.* ask again. **back traet, back treat** *n.* second evening's entertainment of an Orkney wedding.

backer *v.* obstruct, hinder. **backereen** *n.* setback. *'This cowld weather's gin the crop a right backereen.'* **backerly** *adj.* **1** late. **2** timid, shy. **3** handicapped or slow learning.

baest (plural **baest**) *n.* **1** beast. **2** a cow, a farm animal. **3** cattle.

baet *v.* **1** beat. **2** win, *'Come for a fight beuy tae see whar'll baet.'* **aff the baet** unwell. **tae baet fluiks, tae baet a flackie, tae baet skarfs** to hit one's arms across the chest to warm one's hands.

baffled *adj.* tangled by wind and rain. **baffleen** *n.* flattening by wind and rain, *'The crop's gotten some baffleen.'*

bagse *v.***1** struggle with difficulty through mud etc. **2** stride clumsily, *'Here she is bagsan up the road.'*

bairn *n.* a child. **bairns** used to address friends of any age in this sense. *'Weel bairns, Ah'll hae tae go.'* (the exact equivalent of familiar English *'folks'*). **Bairns, bairns!** What's the world coming to! **bairny, bairnly** *adj.* childlike, used of immature behaviour.

ball *v.* throw.

bank, banks *n.* **1** bank, especially a peat bank face from which the peats are cut. **2** the coastline or edge of a loch eg *The Lyliebanks* along the shore of the Loch of Skaill, Sandwick. **banks** *v.* beach, haul onshore.

bannock, banno, binnack, bunno *n.* a flat cake of flour, oatmeal or bere-meal.

banstickle, branstickle, brandie, bruntie *n.* the stickleback.

bar *n.* grain end of sheaf.

bare *adj.* bare. **bare handed** empty-handed. *'He's no bare-handed'* He's well off. **bare naked** stark naked.

barkit *adj.* coated, covered, *'Yin's just barkit wi dirt.'*

barm *n.* rising agent, the froth of fermenting ale. **barman** *adj.* seething with anger.

batter *n.* stiffness in new linen, cotton, etc. *'Wash the tea tooal and tak the batter oot o hid.'*

bawkie, bockie *n.* **1** a ghost, bogeyman. **2** obstacle, problem, *'He sees bockies everywhar.'*

be *v.* to be. The present tense of the verb *to be* is used for the perfect tense, e.g. *'Ah'm been'* I have been', *'Wir done hid'* 'We have done it.' (notice the subjunctive form of *be*, *'If thoo bees good Ah'll gae thee a sweetie'*) **Ah'll just be.** I'm just coming. **tae let be** to let alone. **tae let be for let be** call it quits, I'll not interfere with you if you don't interfere with me, *'Let be for let be again, as the Harray man said to the crab.'* John Firth, *Reminiscences of an Orkney Parish.*

bee *n.* **1** bee. **2** a fly, especially of the large variety.

beel, bael *v.* fester. **baeleen** *n.* abscess.

beesmilk, beestie-milk *n.* the milk of a cow newly calved. **beesmilk cheese** a rich pudding made from beesmilk.

beezer *n.* something really big or fine, *a beezer o a tractor.*

begood *v.p.t.* began.

Beltane, Beltan *n.* an ancient Celtic fire festival held in May when bonfires were lit on many hills. **Beltan tirls, Beltan ruffle** a period of bad weather at Beltane.

ben *adv.* **tae go ben** to go into the best room of a house. **ben-end, ben-hoose** *n.* the best room of a house.

bend, bain *n.* thick leather for the soles of boots.

bere *n.* bere, a type of barley grown in the north of Scotland, common throughout Europe at one time. **bere-bannock** *n.* a bannock made from ground bere.

berge *n.* a piece of wood projecting from the bottom of a door to prevent rain water being blown in, usually called a **water berge**.

bergel, bergilt(o) *n.* the wrasse.

besom, bisom *n.* **1** a coarse long handled brush. **2** an unpleasant term for a woman.

best-end *n.* the best room in the house. **best kens, best knows** *exclam.* Goodness knows. *'Whar he is noo, best kens.'* *'Best bliss thee'* Bless you.

better *adj.* **1** better. **2** more, *'He hid better or a pail.'* *'I waited and I better waited.'* I waited a long time. **better-like** better-looking, *'He's better like the day.'*

beuy *n.* **1** an expression of surprise, not necessarily addressed to a male. **2** a form of greeting used when addressing a familiar male of any age, *'Weel beuy, whit's deuan the day?'* **Beuys o beuys** Unbelievable! Goodness me!

bi *prep.* by. **bi time** early, *'We got wir crop in bi time the ear.'*

bid *n.* invitation. **bidden** *adj.* invited.

bide *v.p.t.* **bade** *p.p.* **bidden** stay.

big *v.* build. **biggeen** *n.* **1** a building. **2** anything built.

big end, muckle end *n.* the room in the Orkney two-teacher school in which the bigger children are taught.

bigsy *adj.* conceited.

bik, bikko *n.* female dog, bitch.

bing *n.* heap.

birkie *n.* **1** *bonny birkie* said for example, to a child with a dirty face. **2** a nickname given to the people of the Sandwick district of South Ronaldsay.

birl *n.* spin around, *'Me head wis fairly birlan.'*

birny *adj.* **1** cold weather with low humidity and usually with wind. **2** (of land) dried up. **3** (of clothing) coarse.

birr *n.* force, a rapid motion, *'I set tae wi birr and cleaned the whole room.'*

bismar† *n.* beam balance used for weighing small quantities up to approx. 12 kg.

biss, birse *n.* bristle or bristles. *tae get/pit somebody's biss up* to anger someone. **bissy** *adj.* **1** easily roused to anger. **2** tousled, *bissy heid.* **birsable** *adj.* hot tempered.

birt o Yule *n.* first of something, *'Here thoo er, beuy! This can o ale is the birt o Yule.'*

bit *n.* **1** bit. **2** a measure of distance, *a good bit awey.* **bits** a North Ronaldsay sheepmark.

bizzie *n.* byre floor where the cows stood.

bla *v.* blow. *tae bla up* (of the wind) to rise. *a bla o dirt* a boaster.

blackie *n.* a blackbird.

blashy weather *n.* heavy, sleety showers.

blate *adj.* bashful, shy.

blatho *n.* buttermilk.

blether *v.* talk nonsense. *n.* chatterbox. **bletherskate** *n.* someone who talks nonsense.

blibe, bleb *n.* a little blister.

blide *adj.* happy, pleased. *'I'm blide thoo're come.'*

blind-daa *n.* spotted dogfish.

blinder *v.* blind with an especially bright light, or with fine snow. **blindroo** *n.* a blinding snowstorm.

blindie-bockie, blindie-blockie *n.* **1** Blind Man's Buff. **2** someone who has not noticed something right under their nose.

blink *n.* moment, *'Ah'll just bide a blink.'* **blinkie** *n.* a moment.

bliss *v.* bless. *Bliss me! Good bliss me!* Goodness me! **blisseens** *'Blisseens on thee'* You have my blessing. *'Blisseens be wi thee'* a parting greeting.

blitter, plitter, pluiter, plyter *v.* work in water. **blittero** *n.* a muddy mess.

blooro *n.* an argument.

blootered *adj.* very drunk.

blots *n.* the water in which anything is washed **soapy blots** dirty soapy water.

blue-niled *n.* mould. *adj.* mouldy.

bluid *n.* blood. *v.* bleed. **bluidy puddeen** *n.* black pudding. **Bluidy Puddeens** a nickname for the people of Stromness. **bluidy sooker** the horse fly.

bluisk *n.* flash.

bock *v.* vomit.

bogle *v.* **1** (of cattle) bellow. **2** (of children) sob loudly, especially, *boglan and greetan.* **boglan and singan** singing tunelessly like a drunk man.

bonie words *n.* children's prayers.

bonnie *adj.* **1** bonny. **2** dreadful. *'That's a bonnie mess yir made.' 'Yir a bonnie like sight!'* **Bonnie fine hid!** That's all very well by me.

bonxie *n.* the great skua.

boofle *v.* strike, beat, give a 'hammering' to.

booick, booa, buack, buo *n.* a large pimple.

boondie *n.* common sandpiper.

boonie *v. & n.* tidy up.

boorwid (tree), boortree *n.* the elder-tree.

borag, borick, bory, brog *n.* a bradawl.

Borroween Day *n.* April 3rd. On this day people can borrow something and retain it! (April **2**nd. is **Taileen Day**) **Borroween Days** Last days of March if fine or the first days of April if stormy.

bosy *n.* bosom.

box bed *n.* a bed, the three sides and top of which were made of wood.

braa *adj.* **1** brave. **2** fine.

brak *v.p.t.* **brok, bruik** *p.p.* **brakken, brokken** break. *tae brak the back o (something)* to make real progress. **brak oot** bring new land under the plough. **brakken road** a rough farm road. **brakken water** choppy sea. **brokken for neb** (an egg) about to hatch.

brae *n.* hillside or mound.

branks *n.* a bridle or wooden head harness for a cow.

brat, bratto *n.* a coarse apron.

brecks, brakes *n.* uncultivated land.

breeks *n.* trousers. **breek-band** trouser band **breek leg** the leg of a pair of trousers.

breekse *v.reflex.* strain one's muscles, exhaust oneself, *'Ah'll breekse mesael wi aa this fifteen.'* **breeksed, breeket** *adj.* stiff from exertion.

breer *v.*(of corn) sprout, *'The corn's breeran bonnie noo.'* *n.* shoots just showing, *'Yin field's in breer.'* The shoots are just showing in that field.

breid, bread *n.* **1** bread. **2** bannock but only in compounds **bere breid, aet breid.**

breid-band, bridth-band *adv.* side by side.

breist *n.* **1** breast. **2** gable end of house.

brett *v.* roll up. *tae brett ap the sleeves* to roll up the sleeves. *tae brett ap tae somebody* to challenge someone.

breu *n.* liquid mutton etc. has been boiled in.

bride's cog *n.* **1** wooden tub with handles used for drinking. **2** the mixture of drink in the cog.

brig *n.* bridge.

bright-eye *n.* the flower eye-bright.

brigstanes, brigsteens, brigstones *n.* a stone pavement in front of a house.

briz *v.* squeeze.

broch *n.* **1** an Iron Age tower. **2** a halo round the moon. Such a *broch* was a portent of bad weather, the number of stars in the broch being the number of good days to come before the weather broke.

brook *n.* a heap of seaweed on the beach.

browst *n.* a complete brewing of ale, three *kirns* full.

bruck *n.* rubbish. **bruck hole, bruck quarry** a hole or quarry where rubbish is dumped. **brucky hoose** an old building where rubbish is kept. **brucky roo** a rubbish dump. **bruckeen** *n.* a severe bruising, *'He's no wan tae shun a bruckeen.'* He's always ready for a fight. **bruckit** *adj.* hurt. **bruckly** *adj.* (of stones) easily broken, friable. **brucksy** *adj.* untidy, slovenly.

brunt *v.p.p.* burnt.

buckie *n.* **1** the common periwinkle. **2** a nickname for an inhabitant of Gairsay.

buckse *v.* **1** walk through a muddy mess, *'He kam bucksan through the iper.'* **2** butt, *'The coo's bucksed the calf.'* **bucksed** *adj.* soaking wet.

buddo *n.* **1** a term of endearment, addressed to a child or a lady. **2** person, 'character', *'He wes some buddo the day.'* (when worked up into a rage.)

buddum, bodom, bothum *n.* bottom. *v. tae buddum* (of a boat) to ground. **buddum moss** the lowest peat in a peat bank.

buddy *n.* a person, *'This buddy cam oot o the hoose.'* **poor buddy** an ailing person. **man buddy** a man. **wife buddy** a woman.

buil, build *n.* pen for animals. **builsteen** *n.* upright separation stone in a byre.

buiss *n.* mess, hash.

buit *n.* boot. *buit-blekk* boot-polish.

bulder *n.* **1** noisy, rough movement, *'The calfs wir coman in a bulder through the door.'* **2** nonsense, *just a bulder o dirt. v.* blunder about.

bulwand, bullowin *n.* dock stem.

bump light *adj.* unloaded, of boats etc.

bund *v.p.p.* **1** bound. **2** fixed. e.g. of an earthfast stone. **in-bund, boond in** hemmed in, especially of houses.

bung *v.* throw something carelessly into some receptacle, *'Bung hid aal in the shed, min, afore hid gets weet.'*

bunker *n.* draining board of sink.

8

burd *n.* **1** a young seal. **2** the young of a fowl. **burded** *adj.* (of an egg) with chick in.

burn *n.* a stream.

burry tuo *n.* tuft of grass.

busk, buss *n.* **1** bush. **2** a lump or tuft. *a buss o gress.*

but *adv.* in the main living room. **but-end, but-hoose** the main living room in the house. *tae go but* to go to the *but-end.*

by-neem, *n.* nick-name.

by-pit, pit-by *n.* something temporary, *'No need fur a belt, this piece o binder-twine'll deu as a by-pit.'*

byre *n.* a cowshed.

9

C

caa v. 1 call. 2 drive, *'Caa the kye oot o the aets.'* **caa canny** take care. **caa ower** knock down. **caa tae** v. close, *'Caa the door tae.'* n. fuss, *'Whit a caa-tae aboot notheen.'* **caa the tae (in)** trip over something.

cack, keech n. excrement.

caddie, kiddie n. 1 a pet lamb. 2 a call to a lamb. 3 a spoilt child.

caes conj. because. **caes why!** because I felt like doing it!-a child's impertinent reply to the question, *'Why did you do it?'*

caff n. chaff. **caffie bedseck** mattress filled with chaff.

cairn n. a heap of stones.

caisie n. basket made of straw or heather.

caloo n. the long-tailed duck.

can v. can, may, be able to. **canna, canno** cannot. *'He'll no can deu that.'* He will not be able to do that.

carvey n. caraway (seed). Formerly it was common for little bushes of *carvey* to be grown near the door of the Orkney house and used for seasoning food. It was said that evil spirits and *forkie-tails* would not go near *carvey.*

cassied adj. (of stones) built on edge.

cast v.p.t. **cuist** p.p. **cassen** 1 cast. 2 (of animals) abort young. **cast aboot** (of the wind) veer. **cast yowe** n. ewe that has lost its teeth. **cassen** adj. 1 faded, *'That gansey's clean cassen.'* 2 undressed, (to a child) *'Er thoo cassen o thee yet?'*

cat's fur exclam. a nonsense reply given to someone (usually a child) who asks what an adult is making, *'Whit's that for?'* *'Cat's fur.'* **cat's lick** a quick wash.

catabelly, catabella n. hen harrier.

cattie-buckie n. the dog whelk.

catty face, catawhissie, cataface n. the short-eared owl.

cauld adj. cold. **Cauld Kail** the nickname of an inhabitant of Evie parish.

caunglan adj. disagreeing, *'Standan there caunglan when wur aa workan.'*

chaa, chaar egg n. an infertile egg, addled egg.

chackie, chuckie n. the wheatear.

chaest v.p.t. **chaested** chase.

chaet v. cheat. **no chaet for** having more than one's share of something, *'He's no chaet for lugs'* He's got big ears.

chalder, chaldro, chaldrick n. an oyster catcher.

changey adj. (of the weather etc.) changeable.

chant *v.* (of a native) talk in an affected fashion to another native speaker avoiding use of the dialect.

chanty *n.* a chamber pot.

chap *v.* **1** knock, *'He chappid fower or five times at the door and got no reply.'* **2** mash potatoes, *'I like me tatties chappid.'* **3** chop wood, *'Ah'll go and chap twa three sticks for the fire.'* **chappeen tree** potato masher.

chapse, chamse *v.* eat noisily, *'Quite chapsan on yir maet.'*

cheek for chow *adv.* side by side. **cheeky for chow** opposite way round.

cheelders *n.* children.

cheeter *v.* giggle. *cheeteran and laughan* laughing in a muffled way, like children in a classroom.

chilter, childer, cholder *v.* **1** (of moving liquid in a stomach or in a bad egg) make a noise, swash, gurgle. **2** jolt, bump up and down.

chilto *n.* a young girl.

chimley, chimla *n.* chimney.

chingle *n.* shingle. **chingly stone** a small pebble.

chirpan *adj.* **1** soaking wet. **2** mentioning repeatedly, *'I got fed ap wi her chirpan on aboot new wallpaper.'*

chocksie *n.* cow parsley.

choldro *n.* an infertile egg.

claa *n.* setback, *'He's haen a filty claa wi the flu.'*

claek, clank *v.* **1** (of a hen) cackle. **2** gossip.

claes *n.* clothes.

clag *v.* stick. **claggy** *adj.* sticky. **claggered** thickly coated with something sticky.

clam *v.* **1** shut (a door) violently. **2** press together in a small space.

clapshot *n.* potatoes and turnips cooked and mashed together, a traditional Orkney dish.

clart, claert *v.* spread something on thickly, especially *clarted wi gutter.*

clash *v.* **1** clash. **2** gossip. **tae clash doon** to throw oneself down on a seat, *'Don't clash yirsel doon here.'* *n.* **1** a heap. **2** a large woman, *a clash o a wife.* **3** a chat. **4** a heavy shower, *a clash o weet.* **clashmaclavers** idle talk. **clash-pie** a tell-tale.

clatch ap *n.* badly made article, botch up, *'Beuy, thoo're meed a right clatch ap o mendan thee ruif.'*

cleg *n.* horsefly.

clew *n.* small ball of wool.

click *v.* snatch, *'He clickid hid oot o me hand.'*

clim *v.* climb.

climmer *v.* clamber, climb.

clink *n.* & *v.* rivet. **clinkit** *adj.* shrunk.

clipe[1] *v.* tell tales. *n.* telltale.

clipe[2] *v.* strike. *n.* **1** a blow. **2** a leather belt formerly used by teachers to punish children, also called **taas.**

cloor *n.* & *v.* scratch. **cloorer** *n.* cold chisel.

cloot *n.* a cloth. **a tongue that wid clip cloots** sharp tongued individual.

closs *adv.* close. *n.* a narrow passage between two buildings, e.g. *Gunn's Closs.*

cluck *v.* (of a hen) brood. **cluckan hen** a broody hen.

cluiks *n.* **1** claws. **2** hands.

clurt *n.* a big lump, *a great clurt o a thing.*

coat *n.* coat or jacket.

cocks and hens *n.* birds foot trefoil.

cockalowrie *n.* a daisy.

cockly, cogly *adj.* liable to fall, unsteady.

cod, headcod *n.* a pillow. **bilge cod** bilge keel on a boat.

cog *n.* small wooden cask.

cole *v.* heap up (hay). *n.* small stack.

collie, collie-lamp† *n.* old lamp shaped in the form of a small saucer which held fish oil, the wick being the inside of a reed.

come *v.p.t.* **cam, com** *p.p.* **comed** come. **come at** improve, especially of health, *'He's walkan withoot his stick noo, he's fairly coman at.'* **come against 1** abrasive in manner, *an aafil come against kinda cratur.* **2** (of food)disagreeable. **cam in tae words** *'Hid cam intae words'* 'We got around to talking about it.' **come thee wiz (wez)** literally 'come thy ways', a familiar invitation to a friend to enter the house and used in other similar situations.

contar *v.* go against. *'Feth, I never contared him in aa me days.'*

coo *n.* **1** cow (plural **kye**). **2** a shellfish like a large cockle, called *coo* by children who used them in farm games. **coolick** a tuft of hair sticking up on the head. **coo's plirt** cow pat.

cookie *n.* a small leavened slightly sweet bun.

coolie, cool *n.* a woollen cap.

coolter-back, coolter-neb, cooter-neb *n.* razor bill.

coom *n.* dust left after milling **in coom** in fragments.

coom-ceileen *n.* sloping ceiling. **coom-siled** *adj.* (ceiling) lined with boards.

coorse *adj.* coarse, rough.

corbie *n.* **1** a rook. **2** a raven.

corinoy *n.* worried frenzy.

corn *n.* **1** bere. **2** small quantity, *'Jist pit a corn o saalt in the porridge.'*

corrie-handed, corrie-fisted *adj.* left-handed.

coup, coop, cup *v.* tip or spill. **cuppan** pouring with rain.

couples *n.* rafters. **couple-baaks** the cross beams in a roof.

cowe *n.* a large piece of heather pulled up by the root, usually *heather-cowe.*

cowed *adj.* polled, hornless.

cowld *adj.* cold. **cowld-bitten** always feeling the cold.

coze *v.* exchange, swap.

craa *v. & n.* crow.

craa-cruik† *n.* hand winding device for twisting straw into ropes.

craetir *n.* creature, person.

craig *n.* throat.

crappened, croppened *adj.* bent with difficulty in moving. *'Hands croppened wi rheumatise.'*

creepie *n.* a small stool.

creu *n.* small enclosure usually surrounded by walls for animals or for growing vegetables.

croolter, crooner *n.* gurnard.

cruggle, crauggle *v.* crouch down, draw body into small hunched up position.

cruik *n.* **1** crook, especially a hook in an old Orkney fireplace on which to hang pots etc. **2** North Ronaldsay sheep mark. **cruik-tree** *n.* beam from which the **cruik** was suspended.

cruisie† *n.* a small open iron lamp with a rush wick.

cubbie *n.* a woven straw basket for holding peats etc. **Cubbie Roo** a legendary giant who lived in Orkney, his name being invariably associated with big stones. His name derives from a Saga chieftain who lived in Wyre.

cuffy, cuify *adj.* clumsy.

cuil *adj. & v.* cool. *n.* a cold breeze.

cuist see **cast.**

cuithe *n.* coalfish in its second year.

cuitheen *n.* coalfish in its third year or more.

cuits *n.* ankles.

cullya, cullyaw, colyie *n.* a seagull.

curl *v.* **1** curl. **2** roll, *'Curl the ball tae me min.'* **curl-dodie, curly dodie, carl doddie** *n.* wild clover, especially of the red variety.

cut *n.* **1** cut. **2** humour, *'He's in poor cut the day.'*

D

daa *n.* father or grandfather.
dab *n.* **1** the proper or correct thing. *'Beuy, that bit o wid is just the very dab.'* **2** trick. *'I got a dab on him.'* I put one over him.
dad *v.* move noisily. *n.* a blow. *'Gae the shovel a dad and tak the sharn aff hid.'*
dae see **do**.
dainty *adj.* **1** dainty. **2** considerable. *a dainty piece tae walk.*
daeve at *v.* **1** deafen with continuous speech. **2** ask for something persistently.
daldo, dydo *n.* (only in the phrase) *He's me daldo.* He's quite a character.
dander *v. & n.* stroll.
dare *v.* make an impression. *'The metal wis that hard the file nivver dared on hid.'*
day *n.* day. *'Hid'll be the day afore hid'* an indication that something has to be postponed. *'I wis gan tae deu the washing bit I doot hid'll be the day afore hid.'*
dead man's fingers *n.* a type of sea sponge.
deadman's liver *n.* the early purple orchis.
dee *v.* die.
deeskit, daeskit *adj.* **1** exhausted, lazy. **2** dopey, stupid.
deily-thing, deefly-ting *exclam.* nothing at all. **deily-bit** no, not at all.

dell¹ *v.* dig.
dell² *v.* knock into. *'I delled me tae in a ston and trippid.'*
deuless, deuanless *adj.* good-for-nothing. *a kinda deuless critter.*
dickie-doo, diggie-doo *n.* a variant of hide-and-seek. **dickie-doo aroond the skroo** hide-and-seek among the stacks in harvest.
die flooer *n.* ragwort.
differ *v.* differ. *n.* difference.
different *adj.* **1** different. **2** a number of different (people etc). *'Different folk wir sayan he's no weel.'*
dight *v.* clean, tidy. *'I must dight oot the byre afore I go.'* *n.* a clean up, wash. *'Gae thee face a dight afore thoo goes tae the kirk.'*
dilder *v.* **1** shake. *'He wis just dilderan wi the cowld.'* **2** dangle. **3** bounce. (e.g. a child up and down on the knee).
dimmle, demmle *v.* dip a vessel in liquid to scoop it up.
ding *v.p.t.* **dang, dung** bang, knock. *n.* a knock. *'He gid me a right ding.'*
dird *v.* bump along the ground.
dirl *v.* spin round. *n.* **1** a blow. *'Whit a dirl he got on the side o the head.'* **2** a toy windmill. **3** a rough passage. *'We got a right dirl crossan the Firth the day.'*

14

dirt, drit *n*. **1** dirt. **2** the dung of fowls, dogs, cats etc. **3** nonsense. *'Dirt wi thee. Thoo're a blether o dirt, a freck o dirt,'* etc. **4** a mild expletive. *'Ah dirt, Ah'm no gaan.'*

diss *n*. small stack (of hay etc.).

dister, duster *n*. light shower, *a dister o rain.*

divot *n*. a piece of turf.

dizzen *num*. dozen.

do, dae, deu *v.p.t*. **did, duid** *p.p*. **daen, don, duin** do. **don, duin** *adj*. finished. *'Is yir tea don?'* **do** *n*. a joke. *'That wis a right do on him.'*

dochan, dowhan *n*. (bot.) dock. *no worth a dochan* useless

dob *v*. prick, stab.

dolder *v*. **1** shake. **2** amble along.

domelus, domerless *adj*. having no energy, listless.

Dons *n*. a nickname given by Westray people to those islanders whom they believed, because of their colouring, to be descendants of shipwrecked Spanish Armada.

doo *n*. a pigeon. **doo-cot** a dove cot.

dook[1] *v*. drive wooden wedges into a wall to hold nails. *n*. a wooden wedge driven into a wall.

dook[2] *v*. duck. *'Dook thee heid when thoo gyungs through the door.'* *n*. a dip in the water, a bathe, ducking.

doon *adv*. down. **doon-by** down there. **dooncome, dooncomeen** *n*. comedown, loss of face, *'Whit a dooncomeen I got when me ker didno stert ava.'* **dooncomeen** *n*.

sloping road. **doonsitteen** *n*. usually a property or farm which a person gets but has not worked for.

doondie, dundie *n*. **1** a saithe or coalfish in its third or fourth year or a big thin cod. **2** a nickname for an inhabitant of Papa Westray.

Doonie, doon the gates *n*. contenders for **the Ba** who were born in the area from the Market Cross to the Harbour in Kirkwall.

doose *v*. butt.

doot *v*. **1** doubt. *'I doot thoo'll nivver see thee £5 again.'* **2** suspect, be of the opinion, *'I doot hid's gaan tae rain.'*

dore *v*. pester, torment. *Deil dore thee!* a mild curse. **doreen** *n*. curse. *'(A) doreen on thee!'* Confound you! (but in a mild sense).

dort *v*. sulk, (of a bird) shun its nest after its eggs have been touched. *'The eggs are cowld, I doot she's dorted.'* Also used of a ewe which forsakes its lambs or of a dog which is fussy about its food. **tae be in the dorts** to sulk. **dorty** *adj*. **1** (of a plant or vegetable) slow in growing. **2** (of a person) sulky.

dose *n*. **1** a large amount. *'a dose o the cowld'* a heavy cold **2** a large number. *'Whit a dose o folk wis there.'*

dott *v*. become mentally confused, especially with old age. **dottan** *adj*. mentally confused.

doven *v.* numb the senses, make dopey.

dowie *adj.* sickly.

drail *v.* trail behind.

dran bits and hemleens *n.* North Ronaldsay sheepmark.

drap *n. & v.* drop.

dreef *n.* crowd, large number.

dreel *n.* (plural **dreel**) drill or furrow in field.

dreid *v.* dread, suspect. *'I dreid hid's no gaan tae be much o a day.'*

drilt, drittle *v.* dawdle, walk slowly.

driv *n.* fine rain, drizzle, typically a **weet driv.**

drivas *n.* powerful thump. *'He fell wi a drivas.'*

droch, drock *n.* wet state; *in a drock o swaet* saturated in sweat. **drockeen** *n.* a drenching. **drockit, drookid, drookled, draigelt** *adj.* very wet, drenched, *like a drookled rat* soaked to the skin. **drook** *v.* soak.

droo, drooer *n.* thin string-like seaweed.

drooth, drowth *n.* drought. *'Hid's makkan a lot o drooth'* A drying wind is blowing. **droothy, drowthy** *n.* a drunkard. *adj.* addicted to drink.

drucken *p.p.* drunk, drunken.

dry biscuit *n.* a plain biscuit without butter.

duggid *adj.* obstinate.

dunder *v.* make a loud noise. *n.* a loud noise.

dunk *n.* bang, thump. *'Whit a dunk he got.'*

dunnered *adj.* stupefied, dazed (after getting a *dunk* on the head).

dunt *v.* strike. *n.* the blow from such a strike.

dunter *n.* the eider duck.

dwam *n.* swoon, daze. *gaan roond in a dwam* going round in a daze.

dwang *n.* cross bearer used in the construction of an interior wall.

dwine *v.* waste away.

dyve *v.* argue. *'Whit er they dyvan aboot noo?'*

E

ear *n.* year *plural* **ear,** if directly preceded by a numeral e.g. *a hunder ear* but *hunders o ears*

ebb *n.* the foreshore. **ebb maet** shellfish, meat from the ebb.

eccle grass *n.* butter-wort.

ee *num.* one (in phrases) *ee day and every day* every day without fail. *ee wey and aa wey* scattered untidily, *'When the bag fell her errands gaed ee wey and aa wey.'*

eek *v.* add to, *'I eekid a bit in the band o his troosers.'* *n.* an addition.

eeksie-peeksie *adv.* evenly, equally.

een[1] *num.* one. **eens** used as a pronoun for things or people, especially, *eens fae aff,* non-Orcadians living in Orkney. **eence** *adv.* once.

een[2] *n.* eyes.

eerie-orums, veery-orums, veere-ottums *n.* decorations, e.g. carvings in wood.

eetch *n.* heavy axe head.

efter *prep.* after.

elsin *n.* awl.

elt *v.* rub hard into, *'White eltan yin chettleen.'* **eltit** *adj.* matted with, filthy.

emmer goose *n.* the great northern diver.

English Kirk *n.* Scottish Episcopalian Church.

errans *n.* 1 errands. 2 shopping purchases. *'Ah'll hae tae go tae the toon for twa three errans.'*

erse *n.* arse, bottom. **erse aboot face, erse first** back to front. **erseleens** backwards. **ersie-crab** *n.* crab which walks backwards.

Eve *n.* the pale mauve orchid.

exe see **axe.**

17

F

faa¹ *v.* fall.

faa² *n.* internal organs of a slaughtered animal.

face *n.* face. **face-washeen** a telling-off. **afore a face** *adv.* headlong, pell-mell, with great gusto, *'The kye's gaan through the aets afore a face.'* **in a face** systematically. e.g. *'Tak hid in a face'*, an instruction given to a fellow worker e.g. to take sand from a pit in a systematic manner. **set face tae** get down to, tackle. **faceens** *n.* boards round a door or window. **facie** *n.* a small cliff or bank.

faddom *n.* fathom.

fae *prep.* from. *conj.* since, *'He's been coman here fae he wis a boy.'*

faerd *adj.* afraid. **faerd for himsael/hersael** someone persistently concerned about his/her health. **faerdy** a taunt to a coward.

fail *n.* a turf or sod. **faily-dyke, feely-dyke** a wall made from turf. **faily-fight** an old game among boys in which they kicked turfs up with their boots and threw them at an opponent.

fain *v.* trust, *'I dunno fain him.'* *adv.* gladly, disposed to, *'I wud fain tell her I ken aboot hid.'*

fair *adj.* **1** fair. **2** good. *'He got a fair price for his kye.'* **fair tae middleen** slightly above average.

fairly, ferly *adv.* **1** fairly. **2** entirely, *'Thee tyres are fairly done.'* **3** quite. *'fairly fairly'* quite so. **4** really, used as an adverb of emphasis, *'He can fairly run.'*

faireen *n.* small gift, souvenir.

fairnteckle, farranteckle *n.* a freckle.

fang, faung *n.* an extra good bargain.

fankle *n.* twist, mix-up, tangle.

fann *v.* **1** (of powdery snow) blow around. **2** (of the aurora borealis) dance around (a metaphorical use). *n.* a snowdrift.

fantan *adj.* starving hungry.

fantoosh *adj.* fancy, elaborate.

farder *adv.* farther.

farrow *n.* a cow which is not in calf.

feck *n.* strength, effect, *'There no much feck wi this ale.'* **fecked at** *v.p.t.* roused oneself, got round to, *'He said he wad but he never fecked at tae deu hid.'*

feefly *adj.* foolishly clumsy.

feenty, fanty, feedy *adj.* relating to the devil. **feenty-bit, feenty-thing** nothing or not at all.

feereen *n.* the furrow drawn out to mark the *rigs* before ploughing.

feeskid *adj.* (of cheese) green on the ouside.

feet *n.* **1** feet. **2** a foot. (the singular form is not used in Orkney). **feetstep, fitstep** footstep.

fegs *exclam.* faith. *'Weel, fegs, Ah'll hae tae go.'*

fendan *adj.* (of hens) searching for food, foraging.

ferfil *adv.* very, especially *ferfil fine.*

ferry-looper *n.* someone who is not a native of Orkney, someone who arrives by ferry.

fest *v.* secure, hammer down stake of tethered cow. *'Flit yin coo and fest her weel.'*

feth *exclam.* **1** faith. **2** indeed. *'Feth Ah'll baet him yet.'*

fierdy *adj.* strong and able, *'He's gey unfierdy noo.'*

fill *adj.* full, *'Mak sure the bucket's fill.'*

filler *n.* a funnel for filling oil lamps etc.

filty *adj.* filthy.

fimlar crab *n.* a kind of crab.

find (rhymes with English *pinned*) *v.p.t.* **fand, fund** *p.p.* **fund** find.

Fin-men, Finfolk *n.* legendary characters from Orkney folklore. **Finfolkaheem** the winter home of the Fin-folk.

fire *v.* throw. *'Fire yir bike on the cairt and Ah'll gae ye a lift.'* *'I widna trust him as far as I wid fire him.'* I wouldn't trust him at all.

fishie-bee, fish matlo *n.* bluebottle.

fiteetch *n.* adze.

flakkie *n.* mat in front of door to keep out the cold.

flamp *adj.* limp, supple.

flan *v.* gust. *'The wind's in a bad airt, hid's flanan doon the lum.'* *n.* a gust.

flattie *n.* a small flat bottomed boat.

flay *v.* **1** skin. **2** trim the turf off the top of a peat bank, *tae flay a bank.* **flay-the-cat** an old sport in which a child would grab the *twart-backs*, swing his feet up and through his arms and back again, then drop to the ground.

flee *v.p.t.* **fled** fly. *'Hid's weeng wis broken, hid just couldna flee.'* *'I fled tae Aberdeen and than I tuk the train.'* **flee, fleeo** *n.* a fly.

fleenk *v.* take on a strong flavour, *'The butter's fleenkid.'* *n.* a toss, *'Sheu disappeared wi a fleenk o her skirt.'*

fleep *v.* **1** turn a garment etc. inside out. **2** skin. *n.* **1** loose bit of skin. **2** lazy lout, useless person.

fleester[1] *n.* a slight shower. **fleestery** *adj.* showery. *fleestery cloods* light rain clouds.

fleester[2] *v.* peel, come off. *'The paint's aal fleesteran aff the door.'*

fleeter, flitter *n.* **1** something flapping or dangling, *'A great fleeter o skin came off his hand.'* **2** *a fleeter o land* an extent of land. **fleetery** *adj.* hanging in rags.

fleg *v.* frighten. *n.* a fright.

flit *v.* **1** move house. **2** move a tethered animal. *'Ah'll hae tae go and flit the coo I doot.'*

flix *v.* frighten. *n.* a fright.

flooer *n.* 1 flower. 2 flour. **flooery binnock/bunno** a bannock made from flour-meal as distinct from bere-meal or oat-meal.

fluik *n.* 1 a flounder. 2 a nickname for Flotta people. *'Hid wis a fluik's heid.'* It came to nothing.

fly *adj.* sly. *a fly-cup* a cup of tea etc between meals.

flyan storm *n.* a real gale.

flyte *v.* scold, *'Sheu's aye flytan on the bairns.'*

fock *n.* 1 folk, people. 2 parents, *'The fock er livan in Kirkwall noo.'*

foggy *adj.* mossy or spongy (eg of a poor quality peat or a frosted turnip).

follow *v.* accompany, *'Ah'll follow thee home wi a torch.'*

fooshonless *adj.* useless.

foosty *adj.* musty.

footer *v.* 1 work clumsily. 2 impede or hinder. *n.* a clumsy person. **footer aboot** potter, work aimlessly. **footered** *adj.* prevented from doing something. **footery** *adj.* intricate, *'This embroidery's a right footery job.'*

for, fur *prep.* for. 1 *'Why for no ?'* Why not?. *'Whitna for a man's that?'* What man is that? 2 used to express intention or direction, *'I gid in for tae see him.'* *'The cat's for in, will I let her?'*

forbye *adv.* 1 besides. 2 than, *'Hid's better forbye the owld wan.'*

fore *n.* (in phrase) *tae the fore* alive, still in existence.

forkie-tail *n.* an earwig.

fornent, fornenst *prep.* opposite.

forrow dyke *n.* in the North Isles a boundary wall which runs down to the low water mark.

fortune bone *n.* a wish bone.

forty-feeter *n.* centipede.

found, foond *n.* foundation of a building.

foy *n.* a party or other entertainment originally to wish one success on a journey. **Johnsmas Foy** a short programme of readings, folk music etc presented at the time of the St Magnus Festival, a revived use of the word.

fozie *adj.* spongy, as for example a turnip which has been exposed to hard frost.

frapp *n.* tangle, mix up (like a coil of rope).

freck *v.* pretend to be ill, make a fuss. *n.* a pampered child. *'Don't bother wi him, he's just a freck.'* **freckid, frecky** *adj.* (of a child) spoiled. *a freckid thing o bairn.*

frim-froy, frim-frass *exclam.* answer to a child who asks 'Whit's that?'
A frim-froy tae tie tae the tail o a speiran boy.
A frim-frass tae tie tae the tail o a speiran lass.

frootery *n.* witchcraft, something unexplained.

frush *adj.* easily broken, crumbly.

fry *n.* small quantity of fish, usually a gift.

fudsho *n.* meadow vetch.

fuff *n.* 1 a puff of smoke. 2 a small explosion. 3 a short involuntary laugh.

fuffle, feefle *v.* work clumsily.

fuggus *n.* thick smoke, choking atmosphere.

fuily *adj.* foolish. *a fuily thing o boy.*

fun *n.* **1** fun. **2** a joke. *'Hid wis a right fun on him.'*

funder *v.* **1** founder. **2** overfeed an animal.

furr *n.* a furrow.

furtiver *adv.* whatever, in any case, *'Hid'll no work furtiver.'* It won't work no matter how it's done.

furtiverweys at any rate, sometimes heard in the form **furtiverweys** or **no**, *'Furtiverweys or no, me mither pat on the pot.'*

fussy-punds *n.* a kind of grass, *Yorkshire fog.*

fyoltry, feltry *adj.* **1** tattered. **2** unsteady or tottering like a poorly built peatstack.

G

gaa *n.* sun-dog, bit of rainbow before or behind the sun. *weather-gaa.*
'A gaa behind ye needno mind,
A gaa afore, lukk for a roar.
gaan *present participle of* **go**: going.
gab, gob *v.* gossip or talk. *n.* mouth. *gab tae the heels* very talkative.
gab o May, gaps o May *n.* stormy period in April/ May.
gablo, gavlo *n.* a crawling insect, specifically a largish black beetle.
gad see **gid-gad.**
gae¹, gie *v.p.t.* **gaed, gid, geed** *p.p.* **gaen, gin, geen** *pres.part.* **1** give. **2** feed. *gae the kye, hens, cats* etc.
gae² see **go.**
gaed¹, gid, geed *v.p.t.* gave (see **gae**).
gaed², gid, geed *v.p.t.* went (see **go**).
gaen¹, gin, geen *v.p.p.* given (see **gae**).
gaen², gin, geen *v.p.p.* gone (see **go**).
gaether *v.* **1** gather. **2** rake. *gaether the fire* rake the fire.
gafse, gavse *v.* eat hungrily. *n.* a deep bite in an apple etc.
gafter *n.* loud, silly laugh.
gaggle *v.* **1** make a mess. **2** work clumsily and carelessly. *n.* careless work.
gamfer *n.* **1** close misty weather. *a gamfer for snaa.* **2** an apparition.

gams *n.* mouth, jaws. *'Pit that in thee gams!'* Eat up! **gamsmyre** *n.* rubbish, idle talk, *'Dunno listen tae her, hid's just gamsmyre.'*
gan, gaun *v.* stare at in a vacant manner, *'Gaunan aboot him, like a deuk lukkan for tunder.'*
ganner *n.* gander.
gansey *n.* a jersey.
gant *v. & n.* yawn.
gappus, gappis *n.* a fool.
gavel, gavel-end *n.* gable of a house.
gee *n.* mood, notion, fancy. *'He's taen a gee tae go tae the fisheen.'*
gelder, geldro *n.* destruction, ruin. *gaen tae gelder, gaen a-geldro* in ruins.
geo *n.* ravine, sea inlet.
gerteens, gertans *n.* garters, elastic to hold up stockings.
gey *adv.* very. *'Hid's gey bad'* It's very bad.
gibbid *adj.* gutted. *'He luks just like a gibbid herreen.'*
gibbie *n.* a tom cat.
gid-gad, giddy-gad, giddy-goo, gad *exclam.* an expression of disgust eg when looking at a meal which does not appeal to one.
gilder, galder *v.* giggle, especially, *gilderan and laughan.*
gilly *n.* person, used when addressing someone. *'Whar er thoo gaan, gilly?'*

gimmer *n.* a young ewe.
gimmer shell *n.* the scallop.
girn *v.* complain in a whining way.
girny *adj.* (of a child) whining, especially *girnan and greetan.*
girnal *n.* a meal chest.
gis *n.* common-sense, capability (only negative). *'He his no gis at aal.'* He is inept. **gissless** *adj.* inept.
git *v.* get, become. *'Hid's a big cat noo gittan.'* It's becoming a big cat. *'Are you gittan?'* a question frequently asked by Orkney shopkeepers meaning, 'Are you being attended to?'
gizzened *adj.* dried up, especially of a barrel or tub so that there are gaps between the staves.
'Auld sycamore, bruck'd by the world's coorse naevs,
Gizzened by summer suns, an stiff wi rheum.'
David Horne, *'The Sycamore.'*
glab, glam *v.* to snatch. *'He'll glab aal he can get his hands on.'* *n.* a snatch.
glaep *v.* gulp down.
glap *n.* **1** a sudden attack of illness. **2** a chill eg eggs might get *a glap o cowld* if the hen leaves the nest too long. *'Wrap up weel in case thoo gets a glap.'*
gleckit *adj.* foolish.
gled *adj.* glowing, *'Whit a bonnie gled fire.'*
glergis, glurgis *n.* sticky mess.
gless *n.* glass. **glessie-hole** a narrow space about **25** cms between the gable ends of the houses in Kirkwall, so called because it was here where all broken glass was thrown.
glett *n.* temporary lull in a storm.
glinder *v.* peer. *tae go glinderan aboot.*
glisk *n.* **1 a** glimpse. **2** short space of time.
glomer *v.* grope.
gloondie *adj.* greedy, gluttonous.
gloy *n.* cleaned straw for Orkney chair making.
gluff *n.* **1** a sudden blast or puff of wind. **2** a fright. **gluffy** *adj.* unpredictable, *'Yin's a gluffy coo.'*
glupp, gluip *v.* gulp, *'Stop gluppan yir maet.'*
glyed *adv.* off the straight. *'Hid's geen glyed.'*
go, gae, gyung *v.p.t.* **gaed, gid, geed** *p.p.* **gaen, gin, geen** go. *pres.part.* **gaan, gyaan** going.
gock *v.* play a trick on *n.* **1** cuckoo **2** someone fooled by a trick. *'Hinty Gock' 'Gock! Gock!'* April Fool!
godick, guddick *n.* a little rhyme with a double meaning, riddle.
godless *adj.* awful. *'She wis a most godless sight wi that owld coat on.'*
golder, gelder, gulder, galder *v.* **1** laugh loudly **2** shout, make a loud noise. *n.* loud noise. *a great golder o a laugh. a galder o wind cam roond the hoose.*
goldrick *n.* the plaice.
golt, goltie, galt, gat *n.* a male pig, used only of old gelded pigs or of young male pigs.

goo, gue *n.* a stink of any kind, especially the smell of rotten fish.

good *adj.* good. *exclam.* Goodness me! *'Good, hid's here somewey.'* *gaan good-o* going very well. **goodly** *adj.* **1** holy or devout, especially *a goodly buddy.* **2** more than, *'He wis there a goodly meenit.'*

goon *n.* gown. **goonie** *n.* a nightdress.

goosrin *n.* gizzard

gowl *v.* (of a person) bellow, especially *gowl and greet.* *n.* a bellow.

gowster *n.* blast of wind, gale. **gowsterie** *adj.* **1** (of weather) windy. **2** (of a person) loud and talkative.

grabbid *adj.* taken aback, annoyed at missing something. *'Sheu wus some grabbid when aal the bargains wur selt.'*

grain *n.* **1** grain. **2** a small quantity. *a peedie grain.* Also used of space: *'Just move hid a grain.'*

Grand March *n.* the first event at an Orkney wedding reception dance, a kind of ceremonial walk.

grap, grop *n.* rough ground grain for animal feed.

grat see **greet.**

gravit *n.* a scarf.

greennild *n.* mould, particularly on cheese or bread.

greet *v.p.t.* **gret, grat** *p.p.* **gritten** weep, cry.

gret see **greet.**

grice[1] *n.* a young pig (*plural* grice).

grice[2] *n.* the sand gaper shell or smerslin so called because it is shaped like a pig's snout.

grimleens, grimpleens *n.* twilight, dusk.

grink *v.* grunt. *grinkan and groanan* grunting with exertion.

grip *n.* grip (a ditch). **2** a mill lade. **3** a deep cleft in the rocks. **grips** *n.* sheep-fold.

gritten see **greet.**

groal, grool *n.* porridge.

groatie buckie, grotty-buckie *n.* a small cowrie shell.

groby *n.* the common mugwort.

gromo *n.* a pinch of (e.g. salt) but applies to the use of four fingers rather than two.

groo *n.* too much. *groo for a sma wey* overdone.

Grotti Finnie, Grotti Minnie *n.* an ogre or hag.

grue *v.* shiver from cold.

gruelly-belkie *n.* **1** a fat person. **2** a nickname for someone from Sanday. **3** a big pot for porridge.

grullyan *n.* a giant or monster.

grungly *adj.* (of liquid) full of sediment.

grypid *adj.* vexed or disappointed.

guff *n.* an unpleasant smell. **guffan, guffy** *adj.* smelly.

guip *v.* make a fool of someone. *n.* a fool.

gullan, gollan, gowan, gull flooer *n.* the ox-eye daisy.

gully *n.* a big knife eg a carving knife.

gulup *v.* swallow greedily.

gumeral *n.* projecting lower jaw.

gump *n.* hind part of an animal's back.

Gunnie *n.* a hobgoblin. **Gunnie's Hole** the name given to gaps in hills. (In Iceland and Norway, trolls lived in such landscape features.)

guppen, guipin, gowpen *n.* a double handful.

gurr, gur, garr *n.* **1** slime on fish. **2** mucus in the corner of the eye or wax in the ear. **gurry** *adj.* of the eyes having mucus in the corner.

gushel *v.* **1** work carelessly. **2** walk with little apparent control of the feet. *n.* **1** careless work. **2** clumsy, messy person. **gushely** *adj.* messy.

gutsy *adj.* greedy.

gutter *n.* mud.

gy *n.* common sense, competence. *'He haed nae gy at the sea.'*

gyre, geyar *n.* a mythical monster or ogre. **gyre karl** an ogre.

gyro *n.* small part of a field uncultivated because of a slope or marsh.

gyte *adj.* crazy,(frequently *clean gyte.*)

H

haaf† *n.* deep sea.

haal *v.* haul. *haal the boat* beach the boat, haul the boat ashore.

hack *v.* **1** hack. **hackid** having chaps on the skin, '*His hands wir aal hackid.*' **2** cough up phlegm. **hackie, hackie-tooh** *n.* coughed up phlegm. *a hackan cough* a troublesome cough.

hack *n.* the footrest on a tusker. *up to the hack* deeply involved in something.

hackit *adj.* ugly.

had *v.p.t.* **held** *p.p.* **hadden** hold. '*Had gaan then!* ' Carry on! Have it your own way! *Had aff!* Be off! **had at** persevere, keep on with. **had for** make for. **had on 1** hold on. **2** continue a journey. **3** annoy.

had *n.* **1** (of an animal) condition, *in good had* **2** shelter, *tak had for the shooer.* **3** lobster's hidie-hole accessable only at extreme low tides. **4** hold, *gaan bi the had* (of a baby) learning to walk by holding onto things.

hae, hiv *v.p.t.* **hid, haed, heed** *p.p.* **hin, haen, heen** have. '*Hid's ither a hae or a want.*' 'It's either a feast or a famine.'

haems *n.* **1** †part of the collar of a draught horse. **2** wooden triangle for sheep's neck to stop it from wandering. **pit the haems on** curb, keep in order.

haep *n.* heap. **a haep o** many. '*A haep o folk don't like this new regulations.*'

haet *adj.* hot.

haeth *exclam.* faith. '*Haeth Hid's cowld!/weet!*'

haeve *v.* heave, throw a heavy object.

haggis, hags *n.* mess. *tae mak a haggis o something.*

hail, hailie-puckle *v.* hail. '*Hid's fairly haily-pucklan.*' **hailie-puckle, hailie-buckie, hailie-picko** *n.* a hailstone.

hain (on) *v.* save, be careful with. '*Be hainan on the butter noo.*'

hairst *n.* harvest. **hairst blinks** distant flashes of lightning at harvest time. *a hairst sky is no tae feck* a harvest sky isn't always as bad as it looks. **hairst knot** a corn dolly given as a token of love.

haley stone (also **lucky stone**) *n.* the name given to small rounded quartz pebbles in the belief that they had fallen from the sky and were, hence, sacred; they were often concealed in the walls of Orkney houses for good luck (no connection with 'hail'; *haley* here means 'holy').

halfers *adv..* halves, *go halfers wi me.* **halfie** *n.* a half-bottle of whisky. **halfleens, halflins** *adv.* halfway, '*I wis halfleens oot o the window when I stuck.*'

26

hallan *n.* **1** a hen's perch. **2** space above a box-bed.

hammer *n.***1** a crag jutting out from the hillside. (common in placenames eg the *Hammers o Syra Dale* in Firth) **2** hammer. **hammer-baeten** *a hammer-baeten sky* a mackerel sky:-
A *hammer-baeten sky*
Is nither weet nor dry.

hand-deueen *n.* '*Hid's his own hand-deueen.*' It's his own fault; he brought it on himself. **handless** *adj.* appearing to have no hands, inept. '*He's a naafil handless craetir.*' **hand's turn** stroke of work, '*He'll no deu a hand's turn*' He won't do a thing. **handleen** *n.* **1** handling. **2** an unpleasant experience, an ordeal.

handsel, hansel† *n.* a gift. **Handsel Monday** the first Monday after New Year which was traditionally a time for giving gifts in Scotland. **handsel wife**† the woman who gave out gifts at a wedding; in Orkney the gift consisted of a piece of bread and cheese.

hank *v.* coil up.

happid *adj.* wrapped up.

happie-kindunkie *n.* a see-saw.

hark *v.* whisper.

harl *v.* rough cast with lime and small stones (also used in Scotland).

harn *n.* rough cloth.

harrow *n.* harrow *as poor as a harrow* of an animal or person very thin. **harrow teeth broth** very thin soup

hash *n.* a quantity. '*Whit a hash o cars is aboot that hoose.*'

hashie *adj.* **1** (weather) wet and windy. **2** (sea) choppy.

hass *n.* the neck but more particularly the throat. '*I hid a fish bone stuck in me hass.*' **go doon the wrong hass** (of food, drink) go down the wrong way, choke.

hassfang *n.* dogfight.

havers *n.* nonsense.

heather ale *n.* a drink brewed from heather, hops, barm, syrup, ginger and water. **heather berry** crow berry, the most common berry bearing small shrub in Orkney. **heather bleater** the common snipe. **heather-cowe** see **cowe**. **heather lintie** the twite. **heatherie brottick** hairy caterpillar found in the heather.

heather-blether *n.* vanishing islands. A mirage frequently seen in the North Isles of Orkney in the summer.

heck *n.* a barred container for feeding hay/straw etc to animals.

heid *n.* **1** head. '*Thoo'll get thee heid in thee hands (tae play wi).*' You'll be punished severely. **2** hair, '*I must wash me heid.*' **heidie craa** black headed gull. **heidlight** light-headed, dizzy, giddy **heidleens** headlong. **heid rig** land at end of field for turning on when ploughing etc. **heids an traas** head to tail.

Heids o Norway *n.* the mountains of Norway which, in exceptional weather conditions, can be seen from the North Isles of Orkney. This is a type of mirage. (see **heather-blether**).

heel *n.* **1** heel. **2** the end of a loaf of bread. **heels ower heid** head over heels.

heeze, heyse *n.* state of excitement.

Helly Boot *n.* an old name for the island of Damsay.

hell-doors *n.* (in the phrase) *coman aboot the hell-doors* almost finished, used up, *'The tatties is coman aboot the hell-doors.'*

hemleens *n.* North Ronaldsay sheepmark.

hench *n.* hip.

hennie-hoose *n.* chicken house.

hen-pen *n.* **1** hen dung. **2** tail feather. **hen pen dirlo** a toy, a potato with feathers stuck into it thrown into the wind. This is called a **cripple craa** in Westray.

Henry-Noddie, Tammie-Noddie *n.* sleep in the corner of the eye. *'Here comes Henry Noddie.'* said to sleepy children.

herald duck *n.* merganser.

herdie boy, herdie lass, hirdie boy, hirdie lass† *n.* children who in olden days were permitted to finish the school year on May 12th. so that they could herd cattle. They continued to herd the cattle till harvest-time.

herto *n.* a pet name for a cow, especially for a cow with a white patch (heart) on its forehead.

heys, hise *n.* a tossing about, *'He'll git a good heys on the Pentland (Firth) the day.'* **hise** *v.* hoist.

heysk *adj.* excited, hysterical.

hiblin *n.* the cormorant.

hid¹ *pron.* **1** it. **2** there (is). *'Hid's a gren more in the bottle.'* There's a little bit more in the bottle.

hid² see **hae**.

hill *n.* **1** hill. **2** the peat hill. *in the hill* working peat e.g. *'The men's been in the hill aal day.'* **hill-dyke** a turf wall dividing the arable land from the hill pasture land in the old system of agriculture. **hill-sparrow** a meadow pipit. **hill-trow** a fairy who was supposed to live in the hills.

himsael/hersael *pron.* himself/herself.

hin see **hae**.

hinderend *n.* the end, *'Although he promised faithfully, in the hinderend I hid tae deu hid mesael.'*

hing *v.* hang. *hingan on a (lang) face, hingan a lip like a mitherless foal* looking glum or doleful. *hingan taegither* very ill. *n.* a slope, *'Thir's a right hing on that field.'*

hingle *n.* hanging holder for an oil lamp.

hink *v.* twist, *'Ah'm gin an hinkid me back.'*

hinmost, himlest, himnest *adj.* hindmost. **hinmost bird** last of the brood. *'Deil tak the hinmost'* devil take the last.

28

hint, hent *v.* **1** gather, especially potatoes or stones. **2** gather and transport, *'Hint aal that toys ben bairns.'* **3** select into different sizes, *hentan ower tatties.*

hint-side foremost *adv.* back to front.

hintie gock *n.* the name called to an April fool.

hippeen *n.* a nappy.

hipple *v.* limp. **hipple-scotch** hop-scotch.

hippuck *n.* hiccup.

hirple, hipple *v.* walk as a cripple.

his[1]**, is** *pron.* **1** us. *'Whit aboot his, can we no come?'* **2** me (after imperative). *'Gae's hid'* Give me it.

his[2] *v.3rd pers. sing.* has.

hiv see **hae.**

hix *v.* hiccup. *hixan and laughan (greetan)* laughing (crying) uncontrollably.

ho *n.* **1** thē dogfish. **2** a nickname for an inhabitant of Birsay. **ho-egg** the egg case of the dogfish. **ho-mither** basking shark.

hock *v.* dig out. *'He wis sittan on the dyke hockan at a neep'* He was scraping bits out with his front teeth. **hockid** having a gaunt appearance. *'His cheeks wir just hockid.'*

hod *n.* punishment, telling-off, 'what for.' *'Ah'll gae him hod when I see him.'*

hogboon, hog-boy *n.* **1** an elf. **2** a giant. The huge finger-print stone which lay near the present Millquoy in Stenness was allegedly thrown from Hoy by a *hog-boy.*

holm *n.* a small island.

home-aboot *adv.* at home, *'He always bides home-aboot noo.'*

homeward bound *adj.* **1** dilapidated, patched up. *'Beuy, thee trailer's a gey homeward bound kind o fixeen.'* **2** (of stitches) very large.

honey-spot, hinny-spot *n.* a piece of wood fitted to fill up the angle formed by the converging gunwales at either end of a boat.

hoodjiekapiv, hoodjiekapiffle, hoodjiekaboogle *n.* thingama-bob.

hoodie *n.* the hooded crow.

hookers *n. tae sit on the hookers* to squat.

hoop *v.* hope, *'I hoop he'll be the morn.'*

hoosaget, hoosaboot *adv. tae go hoosaget/ hoosaboot* to go visiting.

hornie a children's game in which the devil (or devils) take their place in the middle of a playground or field and others try to run from one end to the other without being caught. If caught, the catcher becomes a devil. **Hornie** a Stronsay goblin.

hornie golach *n.* an earwig.

horra-goose *n.* brent.

horrible, horrid *adv.* very. Used as an intensive e.g. *a horrible bonny bairn* a very pretty child. *horrid fine* very good.

horse *n.* horse. (included because like a number of Orkney words it does not change in the plural, *one horse, two horse*; compare **baest**).

horse-gock *n.* **1** the common snipe. **2** the sound made by the snipe as it power-dives in display flight.

host *v.* cough.

howe¹ *n.* a mound, common in placenames.

howe² *v. & n.* hoe.

howld *v.* hold.

hudjan *adj.* seething, crawling with.

huik, hyuk *n.* **1** large knife shaped like a sickle for cutting crop or turnips. **2** fish-hook. **hyuken** *adj.* cold-bitten, feeling the cold. *'He wis aye sic a hyuken thing, always huddlan ower the fire.'*

huiketty-kruiketty *adv.* in a crooked fashion, in the old riddle:-
Huiketty-kruiketty whar rins thoo? Clippit tail every year - whar speers thoo?
Answer: a stream and its bank (the meadow grass was cut from the bank every year).

humbug *v.* inconvenience, *'Ah'll go an no humbug thee.'*

humlie-band *n.* thong to hold oar for rowing. **hummlan** *adv.* extremely, very. *'Hid's most hummlan cowld the day.'*

humpie backid *adj.* humped backed.

humph *v.* carry, (usually something heavy).

hunder *num.* hundred. There were two hundred measures used in Orkney, the *big hunder* or *long hunder*, 120 or 6 score (a measure common to all Teutonic peoples) and the *sma hunder* which was 5 score. **hundersgrund** ground in which it is possible to plant a hundred and twenty cabbages.

huppidie-kra *adv.* (to carry someone) on one's shoulders.

huppo *n.* a toad. **huppo-stuil** a toadstool.

hurl *v.* **1** hurl. **2** wheel a barrow etc. **3** wheel something in a barrow. *n.* **1** a ride. *'Wid yi like a hurl in me barroo?'* **2** a quick movement or action. *'Gae the kettle a hurl o a boil.'* **hurl barrow, hurl borrow** wheel barrow.

I

i *prep.* a common contraction of *in*, *'Go i the hoose.'*

ill *adj.* **1** ill, *ill wi the no-weels* ill with some unspecified illness. **2** bad, used with the negative to convey the idea *pleasant enough* especially, *'He's no a ill fullo (fellow)'*, *'Hid's no a ill day.'*

ill-answeran *adj.* badly behaved, *'That's a ill-answeran thing o bairn that.'*

ill-at *adv.* astray, come by an accident.

ill-best *adj.* best of a bad lot, best of a poor selection.

ill-luckid *adj.* unlucky.

ill-minted *adj.* mischievous.

ill-nettered *adj.* ill-natured, *as ill-nettered as seut* very awkward.

ill-thraan *adj.* awkward.

ill-trickit *adj.* full of mischief.

ill-triven *adj.* undernourished.

ill-veetrit *adj.* argumentative.

ime *n.* soot on the bottom of a kettle or in the chimney. **imy, imy-lukkan** *adj.* hazy, misty, clouding over *'The sky's gey imy-lukkan.'*

imse, impse *v.* **1** move, get going, budge. **2** be excited. *Henry Noddie, puir ald body, Couldno imse a curlie-doddie.*

in-aboot *adv.* inside, *'Bide in-aboot bairns till that man goes by.'* **in-time** the end of break time in some Orkney primary schools.

in-toed pigeon-toed. **inby** *adv.* inside, further in.

intak *n.* fraud, cheat. *'That sale in the toon wis a right intak.'*

iper *n.* midden ooze.

ither *adj.* **1** other. **2** else, *'Whit ither could a body deu?'* **nothing ither** said by a shopkeeper when he means *'Would you like anything else?'* **nothing ither fur 'id** no other course of action, *'When me car broke doon, there wis nothing ither fur 'id bit tae go an git me bike.'* *conj.* either. *'Ither yi tak hid or laeve hid - that's yir choice.'*

31

J

jabble *n.* choppy area of water at sea.

jag *n.* injection, innoculation jab.

jalouse *v.* suspect, deduce, infer.

jeck *n.* a large mug, usually made of tin.

jeelie *n.*jelly. **jeelie-jug** a jam jar. **jeelie-piece** a piece of bread spread with jam.

Jeenie-fae-the-neeps *n.* old-fashioned or badly dressed woman.

Jennie-hunder-legs *n.* centipede.

jimp *adj.* sparing, not too much, *'The lent o the wud wus gey jimp.'*

jing-bang *n.* the lot. *the whole jing-bang.*

Johnnie Mainland/Mainlo *n.* a fish, the father-lasher.

Johnsmas Foy see **foy**

jookerie-packerie *n.* dirty work in the sense of underhand dealings.

jubish *adj.* dubious, doubtful (about something).

jummle *v.* mix up, especially sediment in a liquid.

jumpan jecks *n.* small jumping insects found under stones at the beach. see **loopacks.**

K

kae *n.* jackdaw.

kailie-creu, keeliequoy *n.* cabbage plot.

kailieworm *n.* a caterpillar.

karket, karkid *n.* the ox-eyed daisy.

keb, kib *n.* a sheep tick.

kecko, kaiko, kako, kaka see **chocksie**

keek¹ *v.* kick.

keek² *v.* peep, *'I saa her keekan at the window.'*

keel¹ *n.* the back, especially, *on the keel o the back* flat on the back.

keel² *n.* kale, cabbage.

keep, kyeep, tyeep *v.* 1 keep. 2 (with regard to health) fare. *'Hoo are thoo keepan?'* a common greeting to an elderly person. **keepeen** *tae hiv a keepeen on something* wishing to hold on to something for sentimental reasons, *'Na, Ah'll no gae thee that, I hiv a keepeen on hid.'*

keero *n.* native Orkney sheep.

kemp *n.* ragwort.

ken, tyen *v.* know. **kenno, kinno, kyinno, tyinno** *'I kenno'*, I do not know. **kent** *adj.* known *'Hid's grand tae see a kent face.'*

kettle *v.* (of a cat or a rabbit) give birth. **ketleen** *n.* a kitten or the young of a rabbit.

kib *n.* sheep-tick.

kik, kink, keenk *n.* a twist, especially of the neck, *'Ah'm gin me neck a kik.'*

kil *n.* kiln. **kil crack** a flaw in glass, crystal etc., induced in the firing process in a kiln. **Kil Corner** the meeting point of Harbour Road and Junction Road, Kirkwall where a kiln was at one time situated.

kin *n.* family, family relationships. **tae coont kin, tae redd ap kin** to work out family relationships.

kinda, kindo *adv.* rather, to some extent (a very common expression in the dialect). *'Hid's kinda weet the day.'* **kinda middleen** in fairly good health or condition. **kindaweys** after a fashion, *'Are yi feenished wi the hoose?' 'Kindaweys.'*

kippacks *n.* clover

kirn *n.* 1 a butter churn. 2 large cask for brewing ale in. **kirnmilk** butter-milk. **Kirner** a nickname for an inhabitant of Deerness. **Kirnlicker** a nickname for an inhabitant of Stenness.

kirstie-kringlick *n.* a long legged hill spider. When a child found one he would place it on his hand and say this rhyme:-

Kirstie kirstie kringlick
Gae me nave a tinglick
What shall ye for supper hae
Deer, sheer, bret an smeer
Minchmeat sma or nane ava
Kirstie kringlick run awa!
collected by E.W.Marwick.

33

kiss, kizz *exclam.* sound made to chase away a cat.

kist *v.* place in a coffin. **kisteen** *n.* the laying of a dead body in its coffin. *n.* a chest or box.

kit¹, kitt, kittie, kitto, kitta *exclam.* a term used in calling hens.

kit² *n.* the cry of the red grouse, *kit kit kit kit, kabow kabow.* **kittie-come-hame** the cry of the red grouse. The complete song is:-
Kitty come hame (3)
Whit tae dae (3)
Tae baek (3)
Whit in? (3)
A buckyo-yo-yo-yo-yo.

Kithuntling *n.* a monster. Kit Huntling was a legendary character who lived in Birsay.

kittle *v.* tickle. **kittly** *adj.* ticklish.

klanker, klankertonie, klunkertonie *n.* a big jelly fish.

klatter *n.* mess, wreck, *in a klatter* in pieces, wrecked.

kleck *n.* barnacle. **kleck-goose** *n.* **1** barnacle. **2** barnacle goose.

kleppispur *n.* hermit crab.

klepsie girs *n.* butterwort.

klett *n.* a rock, common in placenames.

klick mill *n.* an old type of mill with a small horizontal water wheel. At one time such mills were found all over Europe. There is an example of such a mill near Dounby. The mill makes a distinctive *click* in operation.

kline *v.* spread, smear, usually thickly, *'Kline some butter on the breid.'*
klined ap against leaning against, clinging to, *'He's jist standan there, klined ap against the wa.'*

klow *n.* foot of a cloven hoof.

klowjung *n.* sheep, or people's, normal living territory, *'Whaur thoo jan? Thoo're oot o thee klowjung.'*

klow-sheer *n.* an ear mark on a sheep.

klumbung *n.* clumsy thing or person, *'Yin's a right klumbung o a boat.'*

klunk, glunk *n.* the sound made when swallowing. *v. tae klunk doon* to swallow quickly.

knap *n.* a knob, common in placenames e.g. the *Knap of Howar* is the name given to the original mound on Papa Westray which proved to be the site of the oldest domestic building in Europe.

knicker *v.***1** neigh. **2** giggle.

knock *v.* pound grain. **knockid corn** bere which has been crushed. *kale and knockid corn* was a popular Orkney meal. **knockeen stone** a concave stone in which bere was pounded.

knorro, knurro *n.* a lump, especially from a blow.

knotless threid *n.* aimless, useless person; somebody with nothing to do, *'He's wanderan aroond like a knotless threid.'*

knowe *n.* a mound.

kobos (in the) *adv.* moulting.

koly† *n. koly-lamp* the old lamp shaped in the form of a small saucer which held fish oil, the wick being the inside of a reed.

krans *n.* tap, especially on a wooden barrel.

kringle *v.* twist. *kringle in aside me* (of a mother to a child in bed) cuddle in to me. **kringlo 1** a leather washer. **2** in placenames a well or a little hillock. **kringlos** moving vapours seen above hills on a warm day. **tae see kringlos** to see stars (after a blow on the head). **kringly heided 1** giddy. **2** foolish. **kringly horns** twisted horns.

kroil, kruil *n.* twisted heap. *sittan in a kruil* sitting hunched up.

krome *adj.* hoarse.

krow *v.* crunch, especially with the teeth.

krummo, kromack, kruibo see **gromo.**

kungle, kuggle, kongle, kummle *n.* a lump of stone or rock.

kurnow *n.* the mew of a cat.

kye *n.* cattle.

L

lacer *n.* a lace, (as in shoe lace).

ladeberry *n.* a rocky shelf used as a pier; common in placenames.

lady's hen see **our lady's hen**

laft *n.* a loft.

lagger *v.* cover with any sticky substance, plaster, smear. **laggered** *adj.* covered with mud, paint etc.

laird *n.* a landed proprietor.

laim, leem *n.* pottery.

laldie *n.* **1** zest, 'the works', *gae hid laldie* do something enthusiastically. **2** retribution, telling off, '*She wis fair gaean him laldie for bidan so long at the pub.*'

lambeen snow *n.* snow which falls in April at lambing time.

Lammas Market *n.* the traditional market formerly held in Kirkwall on the second Tuesday of August.

langsam, langersom *adj.* tedious.

lap *n.* a cut on a sheep's ear for the purpose of identification.

lappered, lampered *adj.* (of milk) curdled.

lapster *n.* lobster.

larrie *n.* lorry.

lass *n.* **1** girl. **2** a familiar form of address to a girl, a woman or a female farm animal. **lassie boy** an effeminate boy.

laverock, lavro *n.* the lark. **lavro-high** a child's skipping game.

lay aff *v.* chatter, talk volubly. **lay oot for** *v.* **1** abuse, disparage. **2** hit, wallop.

leapid *adj.* **1** overcome with heat. **2** scalded. **3** '*Me skin's aal leapid*', used to describe the appearance of the skin after a bandage has been removed.

leavo *exclam.* in the game of hide and seek, the child called out '*Leavo!*' when he was hidden.

leet *v.* **1** disclose, *never leet* don't say it to anyone. **2** pay attention, take heed, '*He wis bad tae thee? Never leet, thoo'll be bigger than him some day.*'

lendie bit *exclam.* not at all! **lends metters, lendie odds** Who cares! Forget it! So what!

lerblade, lerbladeen *n.* the cormorant.

let *n.* abatement, with reference to weather, '*Thir's no let in this weather at aal.*' **let on** *v.* tell, but only used negatively in a secret conversation, '*Never let on.*'

lether, ledder *n.* ladder.

letter-fly *n.* any small moth found in the house.

lew *adj.* lukewarm.

ley[1] *n.* grassland.

ley[2]**, leys** *n.* place for hauling up boats.

lice and nits *n.* a mixture of grey and white wool, *a lice and nits jersey*, see **parago.**

lick *n.* pace, speed, *'He set aff doon the hill at some lick.'*

life corn *n.* a temporary and involuntary twitching of the eyelid.

light (on) *v.* attack, *'The boy lighted on him on the wey home.'*

lightsome *adj.* cheerful, pleasant.

like *adj. & adv.* **1** like. **2** alike, *'My, thir aafil like'* (speaking of brothers for example who look alike). **3** looking, *'My thir aafil like,'* referring to the same brothers who are shabbily dressed! **Whit like?** or **Whit like the day?** 'How are you?' or 'How are you today?' a common Orkney greeting. **the like** such a thing. *'Ah'm never seen the like.'*

liken *adv.* likely. *'He hid climmered so high he wis liken tae fa.'*

limiter *n.* lame or crippled person or animal.

limmer *n.* derogatory term for a woman.

limpet, lempit *n.* **1** a limpet. **2** nickname for an inhabitant of Stronsay.

limro *n.* phosphorescence on objects in the open air and caused by unusual atmospheric conditions.

links *n.* sandy ridges near the sea.

lintie, linto, lintick, lintie-white *n.* the linnet.

lippan *adj.* of a bucket etc full to the brim.

lippen, litten *v.* expect. **lippen on** to chance upon.

lipper *v.* **1** spill over the edge (of water in a bucket etc). **2** jump up, of little waves in a tideway. *n.* a ripple in a tideway. *lipperan full* spilling over the edge.

lirk *n.* a fold in cloth.

lispund† *n.* old weight, approx 12.5 Kg.

lithie *n.* a piece of wood fixed firmly across the corner of a byre and to which a cow band was attached.

liv *n.* the palm of the hand.

loan *n.* lane, roadway.

lock *n.* a quantity or number. *'My there wis a lock o folk there.'*

loff *n.* (plural **loff**) a loaf of bread (*breid* is used only to describe bannocks eg *bere breid, flooery breid, aetbreid*). **loffie saps** a kind of pudding made of bread soaked in warm milk and sweetened with sugar.

lokkars *exclam.* goodness! *'Lokkars me!' 'Lokkars daisy!.'*

loom, loomie *n.* the red-throated diver.

loons *n.* marshland.

loop, loup *v.* jump. **loopacks** *n.* small jumping insects found under stones at the beach. **looper** a sheep which has jumped over the wall from the beach on to the arable land (North Ronaldsay).

loots, louts *n.* milk which has gone sour.

loshans me *exclam.* goodness me! **losh seks** goodness me!

lowe *v.* burn with a flame. *n.* a flame. **tae pit/set lowe tae** to set on fire.

lowrie *n.* **1** the pollack. **2** a small cod.

lowse *v.* loosen. *adj.* loose. **lowse weather** unsettled weather. **lowseen time** end of day's work.

luck penny *n.* a sum of money given for luck. **luck stone** a small red sandstone charm with a hole in it which was tied to the old Orkney plough.

Luckie Minnie *n.* a witch, a name formerly used to frighten children. **Luckie Minnie's oo** bog cotton. The white socks worn formerly by the Orkney bride were traditionally knitted from this material.

lug *n.* **1** the ear, *'He's no chaet for lugs'* He has big ears. *'I widna gae hid lug room'*, I wouldn't listen to that. *'He's fairly layan ap his lugs.'* He's listening attentively to something which does not concern him. **2** that part of a bucket to which the handle is attached. **lugget** *n.* a slap on the ear with the palm of the hand.

luk *v.* look. *tae luk aboot* to take heed. *'Thoo better luk aboot thee beuy.'*

lum *n.* chimney pot or vent. **lum hat** a top hat like a chimney.

lunder, linner *v.* **1** strike heavily. **2** walk noisily. *n.* **1** a heavy blow. (also **lander**). **2** a gust of wind.

lusto *exclam.* Look! *'Lusto whar's coman ap the road.'*

lye, green-lye *n.* green growth in water.

lyper *n.* a horrible mess.

lyre, lyrie, leero *n.* **1** the manx shearwater. **2** a nickname for the people of Walls on the island of Hoy.

lyter *n.* litter, used also of chickens, *a lyter o chickens.*

M

maa¹, meh v. (of sheep) bleat. n. **1** a bleat. **2** an enticing call to a lamb.

maa² n. a sea-gull.

maagse, mogse v. walk with difficulty through deep mud. n. thick mud.

maal n. heavy hammer for driving fence posts.

maalie n. a marble.

mad adj. **1** mad. **2** angry. **mad fur** keen on, '*He's aafil mad fur this snooker on television.*'

madrom n. anger.

mae n. a sand dune or stretch of sand.

mael n. meal (oatmeal etc.) **maely puddeen** white pudding **maely tattie** a potato which bursts its skin when boiled and has a *mealy* consistency.

maet n. **1** meat. **2** food. v. give food to animals. *tae maet the kye.*

maggie-hunder-legs/feet n. centipede.

Mairch n. March.

mairch n. boundary. **mairch stone** boundary stone.

maith n. maggot.

maithe, maisan, meeo, meeth, meethe, meethis n. a point on land used by fishermen to mark or establish their position at sea.

makk v.p.t. **meed** p.p. **meed** make. '*Makk thee supper*' Have your supper. **makk weet** rain. **makk (fur) home** head home. **makk on, makk a deu** pretend. **makkadeu** n. pretence, deception. **makkie up** a tune composed on the spur of the moment.

mallimak, mallduck n. fulmar petrel.

man v. must, have to.

man-buddie n. a man. '*I don't think thir's a man-buddy aboot the hoose at aal.*' **Men's Ba** the ball game played by male adults in Kirkwall.

manse n. the dwelling house of the minister of a church.

Mansemas† n. the feast of St Magnus traditionally celebrated in Orkney and Shetland on 16 April and 13 December.

Mansie n. **1** the popular form of the personal name *Magnus*. **2** in Caithness a nickname for an Orcadian, *a boat load o Mansies.*

market n. **1** market. **2** a fair e.g. Lammas Market.

marr n. an equal, matching one of a pair.

marsgrim, marskamo, maskamo n. the angler fish.

mart n. **1** building used for agricultural sales. **2** agricultural sale.

mask v. brew or infuse tea.

39

matlo *n.* a fly, especially a blue-bottle. **sharnie matlo** a dung fly. **horse matlo** a horse fly.

ma'trass *n.* mattress.

mavis *n.* songthrush.

maxie (the) *n.* myxomatosis in rabbits. **maxie** *adj.* a rabbit with myxomatosis, *a maxie rabbit.*

me *pron.* 1 me. 2 my. *'Tak me claes here.'* 3 myself, *'I think Ah'll go and wash me afore I go tae bed.'* **mesael** *pron.* myself.

meedow *n.* 1 meadow. 2 a stretch of marshy ground where at one time hay was cut. **meedow hay** hay cut from a meadow.

meet *v.p.t.* **met** *p.p.* **mitten** meet.

meeter, metter *n.* 1 matter. 2 pus in a boil or pimple.

mense *n.* a large quantity of something. *a mense o cars.*

Merran Da's Cat *n.* *'He's taen ap wi ither company like Merran Da's Cat.'* *Merran Da* was perhaps an old word for a witch. A mound (now flattened) in Sanday was called *Kro Merran Deem* and the belief was held that a witch was buried there. *Lucky Merran* was a Shetland witch; compare **Luckie Minnie.**

Merry-Dancers *n.* 1 aurora borealis or the Northern lights. 2 a nickname for the people of the parish of Stenness.

messages *n.* shopping. *'I always go for messages on a Thursday.'*

messigate, messagate, messiegate *n.* the right-of-way to a church.

mester *n.* 1 master. 2 headmaster of a small school. 3 mastery, *'He hid the mester o him in the fight.'* *adj.* large, special. **Mester-ship** a huge vessel about which many tales are told in Orkney legend. Legend has it that the first two men who landed on the moon were Orkneymen. They were two sailors who were reefing the sails in a storm and were thrown on to the moon when the top gallant mast of the *mester-ship* struck it!

metticks, mettos, mettoos *n.* 1 a plant or weed, sand-sedge, growing on sand dunes with thick roots running along underground. 2 couch grass.

metteen *n.* 1 a grain of corn. 2 a tea leaf. 3 small thing. *no wan metteen* not one little piece.

Mey *n.* **Mey-bird** *n.* the whimbrel, a spring and autumn migrant, nesting in late May/early June. **Mey-flooer** primrose. **Mey-term** traditionally (and legally) the Scottish year was divided into four terms. The May term and the November term are best known because it was at these times that contracts ended and people could move house or **flit.**

middeen *n.* midden.

middle *v.* interfere. **middlan** *adj.* meddlesome.

mighty *exclam.* a remark indicating surprise: also *'Mighty me!'* *'My mighty'*, or *'My mighty be here.'*

mildroo, miracle *n.* phosphorescence.

mind *v.* remember. *n.* mind. *'Ah'm aff the mind o hid'* I've changed my mind about it. **mindeen 1** remembrance. *no in me mindeen* not that I can recall. **2** small present. **mindless** *adj.* forgetful. *'That's wan mindless thing.'*

mine's *pron.* mine, in children's language. *'Whar's shoes is this?' 'Mine's.'*

mire snipe *n.* the snipe.

mirk *n.* darkness.

mirr *v.* tingle (eg of a leg which has been 'sleeping'). *mirran wi madrom* shaking with rage.

mirren *n.* red grouse. see **moorhen**.

misacker *v.* damage.

misanter *n.* mischance, accident.

misca *v.* **1** miscall. **2** speak ill of someone.

miss *n.* **1** miss. **2** a loss. *'Whit a miss Bella's gan tae be in the shop.'*

mither *n.* mother. **mither's bairn** a spoilt child. **mither naked** stark naked, naked as at birth. **Mither o the Sea** the spirit of the sea, in folk mythology. She invariably won the Spring battle with **Terran** and thus ensured the return of Summer and the cycle of life. **mither wit** common sense.

mitten see **meet**.

mittle *v.* injure severely (eg to hack someone's shins in a game of football).

mixter-maxter *n.* a jumble. **mixture o mercies** a number of odd things, *'In this draaer I keep a mixture o mercies.'*

modren *adj.* modern. (compare **pattren**).

mogie, moogan *n.* mitten.

month, munt *n.* (plural **month** if preceded by a numeral) month. (compare **year**).

moogildin, mudyoleen *n.* an ungutted coalfish roasted on hot embers.

moor *n.* a thick blinding snowstorm. *a moor o snow.* *v.* drift, pile up (of snow). **moored wi the cowld** having difficulty in breathing because of a heavy cold.

moor hen *n.* the red grouse. see also **mirren.**

moorit *adj.* brown colour, usually wool.

moose *n.* mouse. *better a moose in the pot than no maet at aal* an injunction to be satisfied with what is available. **moosefa** a mousetrap. **moosie-haak** a kestrel. **moose-pea** purple vetch. **moose-wab** a cobweb.

moosened, mosened *adj.* musty (of hay, bread etc).

mooth *n.* mouth. **moothie** a mouth organ. **moothless** *adj.* having little conversation. *an aafil moothless cratur.*

moppie, moppit *n.* a child's word for a rabbit.

morefare, morefa *adj.* preferable. *'Hid wid be morefare if yi cleaned up yir room.'* It would be better etc.

morn (the) *n.* tomorrow. **the morn's morneen** tomorrow morning. **the morn's night** tomorrow evening. *'Here the day and awey the morn'*, said of an unreliable character.

41

moss *n.* **1** moss. **2** moorland. **paet moss** a piece of ground where peat can be cut. **upper moss** the upper peat. **lower moss** or **buddum moss** the lower peat in the peat bank.

mostleens *adv.* for the most part.

mozie, mozed *adj.* mouldy, decayed.

muck *v.* clean out a byre. **muckhole** the hole at the end of the byre through which dung was thrown.

muckle *adj.* big. *n.* much, especially in the negative sense *no muckle.* **Muckle Supper** a harvest home feast.

mudge *v.* move, shift.

mudjo, mudjick, mudjie *n.* a midge.

muggrofu, muggatie-fu, muggrie *n.* misty, drizzling weather. **muggrafu** a dowdy colour.

muify *adj.* humid, stuffy, sultry.

muild *n.* earth, soil, mould.

muiro *n.* earwig.

mulder *v.* crumble. **mulders** *n.* crumbs.

mull(s) *n.* **1** (of an animal) lip(s). **2** (jokingly) a person's mouth. **3** a headland (as in Mull Head, Deerness). **mullsan** *adj.* pouting, *'He's fairly hingan his mulls the day'* He's in a bad temper.

mullar, millar *n.* gravel beach.

mullie-fustered *adj.* smashed to pieces.

mummie *n.* small fragments. *'The cup just gid in mummie.'*

mump *v.* grumble, sulk. **mumpan and moanan** complaining bitterly.

murder, merter *v.* bruise, *'Me leg wis aal murdered.'* **murdered blood** congealed blood.

myro(o), morrow *n.* an ant. **myroo nest** an ant's nest.

N

na¹, na na *exclam.* no. naa definitely not, frequently pronounced with a tremor in the voice to give a sound not unlike the bleat of a sheep!

na², no *adv.* not (but only after auxiliary verbs), '*He didna see me.*' '*He couldno come.*'

naafil *adj.* awful, dreadful, where aafil picks up the *n* of the preceding indefinite article. '*Whit a naafil wey o workeen.*' In some cases the *a* of the indefinite article is completely lost, '*Naafil o folk here, min*'; the indefinite article *an* is normally never used before a vowel in Orkney dialect, *aafil* being, apparently, the sole and unaccountable exception. (*naafil* is not used in the North Isles).

nacket *n.* small child, mischievous child.

nae *exclam.* no. naebody, naebothy, neebody nobody. naethin, neetheen nothing.

nail-cowld *n.* extreme pain, particularly in the finger nails after prolonged exposure to cold.

nap *n.* sharp knock, *a nap on the heid. v.* strike sharply.

narleens *adv.* nearly.

nauran *adj.* (of dogs) growling.

nave *n.* 1 the fist. 2 a handful. 3 the handgrip of an oar. navefu handful.

near *prep.* near. *adv.* nearly. nearaboot almost, '*Good! He nearaboot dung me doon wi his bike whin he cam roond the corner.*' near-begaan stingy, mean. nearhand close at hand. nearmost nearest.

neb *n.* beak. *pickan for neb* used of chickens just about to hatch. nebbid moose a shrew. neb-cloot a handkerchief.

neebor *n.* 1 neighbour. 2 one of a pair. '*Here's wan shoe furtiver, noo whar's the neebor o har?*' neeborless *adj.* odd, *neeborless socks.*

needles and preens *n.* 'pins and needles' an example of many inverted phrases found in Orkney.

neem *n.* name.

neep *n.* a turnip. *v.* give *neeps* to. '*Ah'll just go and neep the kye first.*'

neester *v.* 1 snigger. 2 (of a door) creak, (of a new cheese) squeak.

nepkyin, neptyan *n.* headsquare.

nert *n.* very little, '*Ah'm no hungry, juist jay me a nert o yin chaek.*'

netral *adj.* natural. netral girse natural grass.

netteen wire *n.* wire netting.

Neuar-day *n.* New Year's Day. Neuar-time New Year time. The first few days of the New Year.

newsan *adj.* gossiping.

next night *n.* tomorrow night. *'Ah'll come ower next night.'*

nick *v.* **1** (of a bone or joint) crack. **2** twist (and hurt) the neck. *n.* a crack.

nickum *n.* a little brat.

nilded, niled *adj.* mouldy.

nile *n.* the plug used for the **nile-hole** which drains water out of the boat.

nimms, nimm-nimms *n.* good things to eat, used only by children when looking at tasty food or by a parent encouraging a child to eat, *'Come on noo bairn, nimm-nimms.'* **nimmie goods** an expression used by a mother when feeding a baby solid food.

nippit *adj.* **1** (of a person) curt, sharp-spoken. **2** (of a measure) barely enough, *'Hid wus supposed tae be a unce o taebakki but hid wus a bit nippit.'*

nirls *n.* chicken pox.

nither *conj.* neither. *'Hid's nither tae me or fae me.'* It makes no difference.

nitteran *adj.* grumbling.

niver, nivver *adv.* never. **niver a ken I** I don't know. **nivver-spaek** frequently said in reply to an obvious statement, (approximately the English equivalent of *Well do I know it!*). **nivver wis hid ither** a reply to a statement indicating that things have not changed. *'Hid's a naafil maes aboot that ferm.' 'Niver wis hid ither!.'*

nizzan *adj.* staring, *'Whit er thoo nizzan at me fur?'*

no *exclam.* no. *adv.* not. *Ah'm no gaan.* I'm not going. Often used in dialect to express an opposite meaning e.g. *'Hid's no a ill day,'* It's quite a nice day. **tae kenno** not to know, usually *'I kenno'* I don't know. **notheen** nothing.

noo *adv.* now. **noo and sae** in indifferent health or condition.

nor *conj.* or. *'Hid wis far bigger nor hid's noo.'*

normous *n.* a large number. *'Thir wis normous o folk there.' 'They wir a normous o folk there.'* (a corruption of *enormous*; compare **mense**).

Norn *n.* the old language of Orkney. **nornaway, nornie** *adj.* **1** awkward. **2** old fashioned.

Nort *n.* north. *'The wind's gin roond tae the nort.'*

Norwast (The) *n.* **1** North-west. **2** the Davis Straits, Greenland. (a term from the whaling days). **Nor-waster** a special type of sea-chest used by Orkneymen who went whaling to the *Norwast.*

notion *n.* liking or affection (for someone) *'I think he his a notion in her.'*

noust *n.* a scooped out hollow near the beach where boats are left in the winter.

nout *n.* **1** an ox. **2** a fool.

Nuckelavee *n.* a sea monster which features in Orkney legend.

nuggle *n.* the water horse, a fabled animal associated with water. It often grazed on the banks of burns and lochs and when someone was tempted to have a ride on its back the animal galloped into the water and drowned its rider.

nutheran *adj.* humming or trying to sing.

nyaff *n.* insignificant person, somebody not worth bothering about.

nyarm *v.* (of a cat) yowl.

nyavse, namse *v.* chew at, gnaw.

nyow *v.* mew. '*Peety help them thit baroos the cat's dish for hid's aye nyowan.*' Pity help those who borrow the cat's dish for it's always mewing. (said of anyone who harps on about something which everyone would wish forgotten).

nyuik, nuik *n.* nook, small enclosed space. **Neuketineuks** a lane in Kirkwall near the foot of Wellington Street.

O

o *prep.* of. in telling time, '*Hid's five meenits o two.*'

obstrapulous *adj.* obstreperous.

oddle, oddler *n.* the channel which runs through the middle of a byre. **oddle-hole, oddler-hole** the hole in the end of the byre through which the urine is drained away.

offer *v.* make as if to, threaten to. '*The engine's offeran tae fire.*'

on *prep.* **1** on. '*My whit a sea's on the day*' There's a heavy sea running. **2** at. *gaan oot on the night* going out at night (e.g. of a farmer attending to a calving cow). **on a time** now and then. **on-gaans, on-goeens** goings-on, rowdy behaviour. **on-pit 1** an inversion of **pit-on. 2** clothing. '*Anything will deu for a on-pit.*'

ony *adj.* any.

oo *n.* wool. **ooen** *adj.* woollen.

oobie† *n.* part of the old Orkney kitchen.

oot *prep. & adv.* out. **oot-aboot** out and around, '*Wi the fine weather grandad can go oot-aboot again and that's lightsome for him.*' **oot taed, oot-aboot-taed, oot-feeted** splay footed. **oot-be-telled** outrageous, beyond belief, '*The wark yin bairns is wurkan is jist oot-be-telled.*' **ootfa** downpour. **oot-mochted** exhausted. **oot o the wey** out of the way. *no oot o the wey* (of price) reasonable, '*£2 for that piece o maet is no oot o the wey.*' **ootrug** an outward current. **ootside-in** inside-out. **oot-tak** substance, '*Thir's no muckle oot-tak in that.*'

or *prep.* **1** or. **2** than. *bigger or.* **3** before. '*I doot hid'll rain or night.*'

ossigar (in) *adv.* **1** (of hens) moulting. **2** (of a person) down at heel.

Our Lady's hen *n.* the lark in Orkney but elsewhere *the wren.*

ower *prep.* over. *adv.* rather, '*Sheu wis standan ower closs tae the fire.*' **ower-gaen** over-run. '*Me gairdeen's ower-gaen wi weeds.*' **ower-gyaan** clumsy and hurried, '*Sheu wis that ower-gyaan I kent fine sheu wad knock hid doon as sheu gaed by.*' **ower-weel** satisfactory. '*Oh hid's ower-weel.*' **ower-weel hid** that's alright by me. **ower-weel kent** well known, in a disparaging sense. **ower-end** to set on end. **owers** *n.* **1** what is left over. **2** more than is required. **ower** *v.* overcome, to get over. '*Wir owered the 'flu for a mercy*'.

46

owld *adj.* **1** old. **2** a disrespectful term for anyone regardless of age. *'There's owld Garson gan tae the hill.'* **Owld Neuar Day** (Old New Year's Day) the 13th of January. **Owld Christmas Day** the 6th of January.

owse *v.* bale water out of a boat, etc.

owsin *n.* ox, stot.

oxies *n.* oxen.

oxter *n.* armpit. *v.* shift, move, *'Oxter hid ower a bit.'*

oyce, uiss *n.* a small salt water lagoon trapped behind a shingle spit, a tidal estuary.

P

paalo, pallack *n.* **1** porpoise. **2** nickname for a short fat person.

paan *n.* curtain below or above box-bed.

pace, paes *n.* pace. The distance of one step, still used as a measure of distance among older people. (One of a number of Orkney words which do not change in the plural e.g. *fower pace*; compare **horse**).

paddo, paddock *n.* **1** a toad. **2** a term of abuse used as in English *toad!* **paddo-saets** toadstools.

paece *n.* peace. *'Tak paece on thee'*, calm down. *'Sit a-paece!' 'Bide a-paece!'* sit still.

paet *n.* **1** peat. **2** a block of peat. **3** the furrow turned over by the plough. **paet bank** a place from which peat is dug. **tae cut paets** (English to cut peat). **three paet deep** the depth of three standard peats. **paet-muild** peat crumbled to dust, potting compost. **tae pit a paet on the fire** to cause trouble.

parago *n.* mixture of grey and white wool.

partan *n.* the edible crab. *as fu as a partan* absolutely full. **partan-taed** in-toed.

parteeclar *adj.* **1** particular. **2** excellent. *just parteeclar* speaking of the weather etc. *adv.* excellently. *'He's gettan on parteeclar efter his operation.'*

past *adv.* past. *'He wis nine past in November'* He had his ninth birthday in November. **tae pit past** to put away.

pasters *n.* the ankles of a horse.

pat see **pit**.

pattle *v.* walk with short steps. **pattled** trodden down e.g. of a damp piece of grass so that mud can be seen through it.

pattren *n.* pattern.

pech *v.* pant.

pedro *n.* game of 'tig'.

pee *adj.* small, as in *pee-ting* something very small.

peedie *adj.* small. **peedie-breeks** a little child. **peedie end** the room in the Orkney two-teacher school in which the infants are taught. **peedie finger** little finger. **peedie gren** (a) a small quantity. **peedie-oddie, peedie-uddie** very small. **peedie-uddie-nert** smallest possible amount. **peedie-weys** carefully, cautiously. (*peedie* is used especially by children to describe small living things).

peel *n.* pail.

peelie-wallie *adj.* sick, feeble, thin, off-colour.

peenie *n.* an apron.
peerie *adj.*formerly the most common word for small in the dialect, it has gradually been overtaken by **peedie** this century but remains firmly fossilised in placenames e.g. **Peerie Sea**. **peerie-folk** fairies. **peerie-orrie** very small. **peerie-snippo** the dunlin. **peerie-whaup** the whimbrel.
peese *v.* (of children) beg persistently in a family situation.
peetie *n.* pity. *tae think (a) peetie o* to pity.
Pelkie *n.* the devil.
pell *n.* a rag or a dirty matted piece of hair hanging from an animal. **pelliehog** a poor ragged sheep which has barely survived the winter. When March was cold and bitter they had a saying in Sanday, *'Mairch said tae April, if yi'll lend me days three, Ah'll mak aa thee pelliehogs tae dee.'*
pellet *n.* uncured sheepskin.
pelt *n.* a blow, *'She got a right pelt on the side o the head.'* **pelter** *v.* hit with stones or snowballs etc.
pelter(s) *n.* **1** rags. **2** dung clinging to an animal's coat **3** matted hair on an animal. **peltry** *adj.* hanging in rags.
peltrie *n.* a number of people, or sheep, whose arrival is unwelcome, *'Bide oot o sight till yin peltrie jung by.'*
pen-gun *n.* a type of pea shooter made from a pen or quill. A piece of turnip is stuck in each end, one piece is forced in with a stick and the compressed air forces the other out, pop-gun style. **gaan on like a pen-gun** talking non-stop.
penny *n.* penny, money. *anything tae mak a penny* anything to earn money. *Every penny's a prisoner.* He's tight-fisted. *He's no wantan a penny.* He has plenty of money. **penny-for-the Pope** at Hallowe'en the children of Stromness go round with their turnip lanterns using this phrase as their begging slogan.
Peolu *n.* the Devil.
perjink *adj.* prim.
pernickety *adj.* precise, fussy.
pey *v.* **1** pay. **2** smack, *'Ah'll pey thee tail.'* I'll smack you on the bottom.
pick *v.* **1** pick. **2** move slowly (e.g. in walking or doing a job), especially *pickan awa*. **3** tap lightly (eg on a window). **pickan for neb** used of chickens just about to hatch. **pickid** (of the hands) chapped through working in cold weather. **pick** *n.* a light tap. **picko, stonie-picko** *n.* the old name for the children's game popularly known as tig. In **high picko** the child had to be touched on the body, in **low picko** on the legs, in **relievie picko** a child had to stand still when touched but could be set free again in a number of ways. **(hailie)-picko** hailstone.
picka, picko *n.* the blenny (Stromness).

49

pickie, pickie-terno *n.* a tern.
Picks *n.* Picts. **Pickie Dyke** any prehistoric earthen wall. **Picks' hoose** a general name for what appears to be any prehistoric dwelling. **Pickie knowe** prehistoric mound.

piece *n.* **1** piece. **2** a piece of bread. **3** packed lunch. **4** a distance. *'He lived a piece awey.'* **5** place. *'Ah'm no gaan tae get a car for I hiv no piece tae keep hid.'* **piece-aff** North Ronaldsay sheepmark. **piece-time** break time or interval in the Orkney school. **anypiece** anywhere. **somepiece** somewhere. **wharpiece** where, *'Whar piece are yi gaan?'*

pie-hole *n.* a hole in leather etc to allow a lace to pass through.

pile *n.* **1** pile. **2** crowd. *'Beuy whit a pile o folk wis there.'*

piltick *n.* a second year coalfish.

pin *v.* run, hurry. *n.* speed. *'Beuy, thoo're gaan at some pin wi thee plooeen the day.'*

pinkie *n.* the little finger. (also known as **winkie**).

pink-peenk *n.* the sound made by water dropping in a bucket etc.

pirl[1] *n.* a little ball of dung of sheep, rabbit etc.

pirl[2] *v.* turn round lightly. **pirlan** the spiralling motion of e.g. a rope running over the gunwale of a boat.

pit *v.p.t.* **pat, pot** *p.p.* **pitten** put. **tae pit mad** to make angry. **tae pit at** to annoy, *'That pits at me.'* **pit fur** send for, *'Pit fur the doctor*

at wance.' 'Pit in thee hand noo' an invitation to start helping oneself (e.g. at a supper table). **pit on** to make an excuse; pretend. **pitten** *p.p.* put. (A pupil noticed another pupil's mistake and allegedly said to the teacher *'He's gin and pitten pitten whar he should hiv pitten put.'*) **pitten aboot** upset or flustered. **pitten tae, teu-pitten** put to (a test), *'He wis right pitten tae, tae baet (beat) him.'* **at-pitten, pitten-at** provoked. **pit the peter on** put a firm stop to something. **pit-by, by-pit** something temporary. *'Hid'll deu as a pit-by.'* **pit-on** excuse, pretence.

pivver *v.* vibrate, shake.

pizzo *n.* **1** mix-up. **2** worked-up state, agitation. *'He wis in sic a pizzo he couldno think whit tae deu next.'*

place *n.* **1** palace. **2** Birsay village, *doon at the Place* i.e. at the Earl's Palace in Birsay.

plantie-creu, plantiequoy *n.* a yard for plants, often **kailie-creu**.

plat, platse *v.* walk around with heavy feet, tramp. *'Sheu wis platsan aboot in the ebb.'*

platt *v.* scald a pig after killing to remove bristles etc. **platteen tub** *n.* large vessel for scalding.

pleenk, plink *n.* weak drink, e.g. tea or beer.

pleep, pleed, pleet, pleeter *v.* **1** whine, make a mournful noise. **2** squeak e.g. of a fatty sausage frying in a pan, *pleepan wi fat.* *n.* **1** a mournful noise. **2** a complaining person. **pleepie** *adj.* complaining. **water-pleep** the snipe.

plester *n.* **1** mess. **2** (of a person) nuisance.

plick *v.* **1** pluck. *tae plick a hen.* **2** pick (fruit). *tae plick at* to tease.

plicko *n.* a torch.

plinkers *n.* eye-lashes, usually *eye plinkers.*

plirt, plurt *n.* a sudden fall or tumble. *tae sit in a plirt* to sit as if one had fallen. **coo's plirt** a cow pad.

plitter, pluitter *v.* work (needlessly) in water, especially of children. *n.* a watery mess or a mess generally.

pliver, plivver *n.* the golden plover.

ploo *v. & n.* plough.

plook *n.* a pimple.

plout *v.* plunge. **plout-kirn** the old type of churn in which butter was made by *plouting* a stick up and down. Milk was used for this process, not cream, the churn being wide at the top unlike the cream churn which was narrow at the top.

plover's page *n.* the jack snipe, dunlin

plowter *v.* walk about in mud or water. *n.* a mess of a job, *'Whit a plowter yir makkan o that.'*

pluck (in the) *adv.* (of hens) in a moulting condition.

plushnie *n.* a catapult.

pock *n.* originally a paper bag or hessian sack but now applied to polythene sacks and bags as well.

pogo *n.* a child's toy made from feathers tied together and released in the wind.

pooch *n.* pocket.

poort *n.* cry baby. **poortsy** *adj.* whining.

pooshon *n.* **1** poison. **2** nasty person. *exclam.* Bother!

poot, pootie *exclam.* call to a pig.

poots *v.* sulk. **pootsie, pootsan** *adj.* pouting, sulking. **tak the poots** sulk.

pottie *n.* putty.

pow *n.* pool (of water etc.)

pownie *n.* pony.

powsted *adj.* exhausted after effort.

pram *n.* small rowing boat.

preen *n.* a pin.

preeve *v.* test a sea area for fish. *n.* such a test.

press *n.* a cupboard.

prinky, prinkan *adj.* conceited.

prog *v.* pierce, stab, prick. *'Please sir, Trevor's just proggid me wi a preen.'*

proper spoken *adj.* speaking English without a hint of dialect.

puckle *n.* a small quantity.

puddeens *n.* **1** intestines. **2** the intestines of the animal filled with meal etc. **Oh, puddeens** *exclam* Oh, bother.

pudyan *n.* a small, fat person.

puggled *adj.* **1** exhausted, tired. **2** broken, ruined. *'Me watch is puggled.'*

puggie *n.* a child's word for stomach.

puiltie, poltie *adj.* fat, stumpy.

pund¹, puind *v.* (of animals) herd, enclose. *n.* enclosure for holding animals.

pund[2] *n.* a pound weight. (N.B. a pound (£) is pronounced as in English.) *'At wan time cheese wis a pound a pund.'*

punder, pundler, pundlar, poundler, punlar† *n.* a large weighing beam formerly used in Orkney.

purdo *n.* unappetising looking food.

purgas, purgis *n.* a disgusting lump (of something), a horrible mess.

purm *n.* a bobbin, reel of thread.

Q

quack *v.* **1** quake. **2** swarm, *'The girnal wis just quackan wi mites.'*

quackoo, whackoo *n.* a quagmire.

quark *v.* **1** swallow noisily, gulp down. **2** cough.

queebeck *n.* the call of the grouse.

quey, queyo *n.* heifer or young cow with first calf.

quill, whull, whullo *n.* small boat with bow and stern shaped the same.

quink *n.* **1** brent. **2** greylag goose. **3** golden-eyed duck.

quite *v.* quit, stop. *'Quite hid, min!.'*

quoy, why *n.* a piece of common pasture enclosed and cultivated, frequent in placenames when, at the end, it is usually pronounced *quee.* e.g. Haquoy, pronounced *Haquee.*

R

raa *adj.* raw.

raan *n.* roe.

race *n.* 1 race. 2 a short trip. '*I gid tae the toon a race.*'

raes *n.* a knot, especially **runnan raes**, a slip knot.

raffle, raeffle *n.* tangle, mix-up.

ragstones *n.* stones set on edge on top of a wall.

rain-goose *n.* the red-throated diver. Its song is:-
> *Mair weet, mair weet*
> *Waur wedder Waur wedder*
(from the belief that the call of the bird was a sign of rain).

raip *n.* 1 rope. 2 specifically the line, usually a piece of twine, stretched above the fireplace on which clothes etc were hung to dry.

rake *v.* stretch out the hands. An old invitation to eat heartily was, '*Rake in yir hand an dinna need a biddeen.*' **rake a had o** grab hold of. **rake on** make amorous advances to; ravish.

rammle-back *n.* a bar in a chimney from which pots were suspended (also known as *rantle-tree*).

ramp *v.* 1 romp. 2 boil vigorously, *rampan and boilan.* **rampan** *adj.* restless, always on the move.

ramse *adj.* 1 rough in behaviour, (e.g. someone pushing in through a door heedless of others.) 2 *(of butter)* rank.

ramstam *adj.* careless, headstrong.

rash *v.* rush. *rashan (and rainan)* pouring with rain.

rattan *n.* rat.

rattle up *v.* build with speed; several cottages in Orkney have this (not very complimentary!) name.

rattle doon *v.* demolish quickly.

rause *v.* praise, '*Rause the fair day at night.*' Wait until night before saying it has been a lovely day in case it rains later.

ravsie *adj.* badly dressed.

red see **reid.**

redd[1] *v.* 1 clear out, tidy up. '*We'll hiv tae redd oot that owld shed ready fur the tatties.*' 2 comb. **redder** *n.* a comb.

redd[2] *n.* speed, '*I kent I war short o time but I could mak nee redd for the bairn waes wi me.*' **reddly** *adj.* quick and competent, *a reddly worker.*

ree *adj.* mad, daft, hysterical.

reek *v.* 1 emit smoke. 2 (of a fire) send smoke into a room. 3 emit strong smell (e.g. urine on clothes). *n.* 1 smoke. 2 stench, '*My whit a reek wi that owld cloot!*' **reek-hole** a hole in the roof of the old Orkney house through which the smoke passed. **reekie brae** there are several such placenames in Orkney where fires were lit to send smoke signals e.g. to request a ferry. (e.g. *Reekie Brae* on Copinsay).

54

reel *n.* reel. *reel o the barn* the last dance at an old Orkney wedding.

reest *v.* dry or cure meat by hanging in smoke. *n.* where meat was hung to *reest.*

reester, roster *n.* a bright roaring fire, *'My whit a reester yir pitten on.'*

reid, red *adj.* red. *n.* poor quality rock used for bottoming roads, *'We'll need tae pit twa loads o red on the paet hill road.'* **reidba** the yolk of an egg. **reid-loon** *reid-loon paet* a peat which burns leaving a red ash. **reidware** seaweed. **reidware cod** an inshore codling; they have a slight reddish colour.

renyie *n.* 1 a sharp pain. 2 a tug, sharp pull.

reshes *n.* rushes.

rex *v.* stretch, especially of the arm. *'Rex in noo and mak thee supper'* a friendly invitation to help oneself.

rheuma'tics (the), rheumatise *n.* rheumatism.

ricketie buckie *n.* a small snail which when pulverised (or cooked in milk) supposedly cured rickets. These snails were (and still are) found round St Tredwell's Chapel in Papa Westray.

rickle *n.* something loosely made or built. **ricklie, rucklie** *adj.* tottering.

rift *v. & n.* belch.

rig *n.* 1 piece of land 5 yards wide. 2 harvest field, *'Beuy, I see thoo're right busy in the rig the day.'*

riggeen *n.* back, *the keel o the riggeen* flat on the back.

right *adj.* 1 right. 2 sound in mind (usually used negatively). *'That boy canna be right.'* *adv.* very. *right good.* **rights** *n.* correct account. *'I never got the rights o hid.'* I never found out the truth.

rine *n.* the cross-shaped fitting which supports an upper millstone.

ringer goose *n.* the shelduck.

rink *n.* twist, *'Ah'm gin me neck a rink.'*

rip *n.* North Ronaldsay sheepmark.

ripe oot *v.* clean out.

rit *v.* cut, slash. *n.* a slit on the ear, used as a sheepmark. **ritteen knife** a very large knife not unlike a scythe but with the opposite edge sharpened, used in peeling the turf off banks and in making the horizontal cuts for the peats.

rither *adv.* rather, in the tongue twister:-

Whither wid yi rither
Ur rither wid yi whither
Hiv a stewed soo's snoot
Ur a soo's snoot stewed?'

ritto, rittock *n.* a black-headed gull. In some parts of Orkney also a tern or a kittiwake.

rive *v.p.t.* **rave** *p.p.* **rivven 1** tear. *'The wid in the deck o the boat is rivven wi the sun.'* **2** tear something away from something else, *'Rive hid min.'* (e.g. when a piece of scaffolding had jammed). **rive at** work hard at. *'Thoo're ferly rivan at the plooen the day.'*

rivlin† *n.* an old type of shoe made of untanned hide.

rone *n.* guttering around eaves, the down pipe from a gutter.

rone moose *n.* the shrew.

roo¹ *v.* make a heap. *n.* a disorderly or messy heap.

roo² *v.* pluck the wool off sheep. **rooed** having the hair or wool removed.

rook *n.* (in phrase) *as thin as a rook* very thin.

rookery *n.* uproar, unrest.

rookle, ruckle *n.* heap, pile. *ruckle o bones* thin, scraggy person or animal.

roop, roup, roap *n.* an auction sale. *v.* rob, steal, plunder.

roove *n. (boat building)* metal washer for use with a nail to make a rivet.

rorie *adj.* (of a colour) bright and garish.

rosit *n.* rosin. **rosit ends** hemp thread prepared with *rosin* for sewing leather.

rost¹, roost *n.* a rough tideway, e.g. Burgar Rost between Evie and Rousay.

rost² *v. & n.* roast. *'He cam oot in a rost o spots'* the body was covered with spots. **rostan** used to describe severe instances of childhood illnesses such as chickenpox etc. *'Beuy she's just rostan wi the maesles.'*

row, rowl *v. & n.* roll.

ruckle *v.* **1** wrinkle. **2** shrug the shoulders.

rudge *v.* (of a boat against a pier) rub and chafe. *n.* the rattle of pebbles on a beach or of mucus in the throat.

rug¹ *n.* wet mist. **ruggie** *adj.* drizzling.

rug² *v.* pull vigorously.

rugfus *adj.* **1** strong. **2** boisterous.

ruif *n.* **1** roof. **2** ceiling (the roof and ceiling were at one time the same thing!)

Rullie *n.* **1** an affectionate name for North Ronaldsay. **Rullie-folk** people born in North Ronaldsay.
> *Tae foreign lands I haed*
> *tae jung,*
> *Tae work for me and mine,*
> *Aald Rullie, tae me deean*
> *day*
> *Me hairt is aulwus thine.*
North Ronaldsay exile.

run *n.* **1** run. **2** a heavy sea. *'Whit a run is on the sea the day.'*

runcho *n.* charlock, wild mustard.

runge *n.* the sound of the sea breaking on the shore.

runnick *n.* a small open drain.

runt *n.* stem, *keel-runt* stem of cabbage.

rysos, rice *n.* brushwood.

S

saa *v.* to sow.

saat, saalt *n.* salt.

sabbid *adj.* soaked.

sae, say *n.* large wooden tub with *lugs* through which a pole was passed to enable it to be carried easily. **sae-bink** a stone bench in the end room of a house on which the *sae* stood with the clean water supply for the household. **sae tree** the pole which was used to carry the *sae*.

saegs, segs *n.* rushes. It was believed that chewing *saeg* leaves was liable to make a child stammer or make him dumb. **saegs, seggie flooers** the wild iris.

sael *pron.* self. *mesael, theesael* etc.

saem, seam *n.* 1 seam. 2 a parting in the hair. **saemer** the narrow flagstone which covers the gap between two roofing flags.

saetro *n.* children's counting-out rhyme e.g. '*Eetle-ottle black bottle*' etc.

saft *adj.* soft.

salor, salur, saller, siller, sellar, seller, sullar *n.* a small room leading off the living room and used as a bedroom. **siller door** the door into such a room.

sam *adj.* same.

sandlark *n.* the sandpiper. **sandlo, sanloo, sinlick** the ringed plover.

sannie-back a kind of flounder.

sand-paet a poor quality peat dug from a shallow moor; such peats were placed at the back of an open hearth fire; they were also burned and the ash used to manure the *plantie-creu*.

san lavro *n.* a skylark. *tae jump san lavro height* to jump very high.

sap *n.* a small quantity, '*Pit a good sap o milk in the bucket.*'

saps *n.* bread mixed with warm milk and sugar given to a child. '*Tak thee saps*' used jocularly to an adult, '*Eat up.*'

sark *n.* 1 a shirt. 2 the black membrane which lines the belly of a fish. **sarkeen** *n.* wooden lining boards for a roof.

saw-bill *n.* the goosander, the red-breasted merganser.

scadman's head, scar-man's head scarriman's head, scardiman's heid *n.* sea-urchin shell.

scad/scarred rocks *n.* rocks with tiny white shells growing on them.

scale duck *n.* the shelduck.

scone *n.* a pancake. *as flat as a scone* absolutely flat.

scoor *n.* scour, diarrhoea.

scootie *n.* the starling.

scooty-allan, scotty-fool *n.* Arctic skua, formerly known as *dirten-allan.*

scottie *n.* the oyster catcher (North Isles only).

scow *n.* a barrel stave. **scows** fragments. *tae lay in scows* to shatter, *'Thir wis notheen bit the scows o the hen left when I got home'* (the rest had been eaten!).

scrat *v.* scratch. **scratto, scratter** *n.* a pot cleaner. The original pot cleaners were made from horse hair or heather.

scrubber† *n.* a flat stone etc dragged over a field to crush clods.

scuddleen claes *n.* second-best clothes, casual wear.

scuffle *v.* destroy weeds between drills with a horse hoe. **scuffler** *n.* the horse hoe used for this.

scunner *v.* 1 sicken, disgust. 2 loath. *n.* something or someone causing disgust. **scunnerous** disgusting. **get a scunner** get more than enough of something. **tak a scunner tae** take a dislike to.

sea-crow *n.* the razorbill. **sea-cubbie** a straw or heather basket for carrying fish. **sea-geese** barnacles which grow on driftwood. **sea parrot** the puffin. **sea-trow** a sea spirit. **sea-uikie** sea scorpion.

seck *n.* a sack. **seckie** *adj.* made of sackcloth. **seckie-bratto** an apron made of sackcloth. **bedseck** *n.* mattress.

seek *adj.* sick. **seekensome, seeknan** *adj.* sickening.

selkie *n.* 1 a grey seal. 2 a nickname for an inhabitant of North Ronaldsay. **selkie-folk** seals capable of transforming themselves into human beings.

semmit, simmet *n.* a vest.

servant lass *n.* a young girl employee, especially on a farm. **servant man** a farm labourer.

sester, sesters *n.* the channel in a byre draining away cattle urine, also known as the *oddle* or *oddler* (almost always used in the plural)

set *v.* 1 set. 2 plant (particularly potatoes), *'We set twa-three dreel o tatties last night.'* **set face tae** get down to, tackle. **set low tae** set on fire. **setteen** sufficient, *a setteen o eggs* eggs to put under a broody hen; *a setteen o tatties,* sufficient for one planting.

Setterday *n.* Saturday. *A silken Setterday affens maks a canvas Monday,* good weather on Saturday seldom lasts till Monday.

seut *n.* soot. *seutie salt's good enough for hairy butter* said of two equally bad things or people brought together. *The ruif's drappan seut.* said when someone is listening in to a conversation.

seven ear o Yule days a very long time. **seven lang and seven short** a very long time.

sha *v.* **1** show. **2** pass by hand, '*Sha me a hammer*' Pass the hammer. '*Sha me see the letter.*' Let me see the letter. *n.* the part of a plant, especially a potato or a turnip, above the ground.

shak *v.* shake. **shakkeen stanes** *n.* small flagstones built into the sidewalls of the barn thrashing floor about 70 cm high and projecting about 12 cm. It was on these stones that handfuls of corn were thrashed to make *gloy.*

shadie *n.* a little. '*He's a shadie better*', '*Move hid ower tae the left a shadie.*'

shaef *n.* **1** sheaf. **2** a slice, *a shaef o loaf.*

shaft *v.* shake. *shaft a naive* shake one's fist.

shald, showld *n.* a shoal in the sea. *adj.* shallow.

shalder, shelder *n.* the oyster catcher.

shankie *n.* the redshank.

share[1] *v.* (of teeth).grind or bare, '*Yin dog's sharan his teeth at me.*'

share[2] *v. p.p.* **shorn. 1** cut peats, corn etc, '*Langskaill sterted tae share the day.*' **2** (of milk) become sour. **aff-shareen** *n.* special meal or *Muckle Supper* to celebrate the end of grain cutting in harvest.

sharg *v.* nag.

sharger *n.* a puny individual. *Hair and nails grow weel tae shargers*, an old saying.

sharn *n.* cow dung but only used of cow dung sticking to something e.g. a shovel or trousers.

sharp *adj.* **1** sharp. **2** (of milk) sour. **sharpeen stone** a whetstone.

sheed *n.* a small field.

shear *n.* North Ronaldsay sheepmark.

shears *n.* scissors.

Sheep-right Day that day on which native sheep were required by local law to be rounded up for counting, shearing, culling etc.

sheer *n.* a slit on an animal's ear as a mark of identification. **sheer moose** a shrew. **sheer tail** the tern.

sheld fowl *n.* the sheld duck.

shellmaleens, sheer-maleens, sheer-mellins, shellmilleens *n.* fragments.

shellweengs, shilweengs *n.* sideboards for cart or trailer.

shepherd's reed *n.* mouth-organ.

sheu *pron.* she.

shilpit *adj.* sour to the taste.

shock *n.* **1** shock. **2** a (paralytic) stroke. *tae tak a shock.*

shoe, sheu *n.* shoe. (the old plural was **shoon, shuin**).

sholt, sholtie *n.* **1** a small horse, usually *Shetland sholt.* **2** a foreshore creature living under stones, the black sand hopper. **3** the common top shell. *adj.* from Shetland; quern stones were usually *Sholtie stones.*

shoogle *v.* shake, totter. **shoogly, shaugly** *adj.* tottering.

shooder, shoother, shudder *n.* **1** shoulder. **2** the edge of a hill, *the shooder o the hill.*

shore-sparrow, shore-teeting *n.* rock pipit. **Shoracks**† an old name for the inhabitants of Kirkwall who lived by the shore, now generally applied to *Doonies.*

short ago, short syne *adv.* recently.

shuit¹ *v.* **1** push, *'Shuit fae thee noo beuy.'* **2** hurry. *'Shuit ower tae Willie for his hammer.'*

shuit², **shut** *v.* (of walls) bulge. *'The wall seems tae be shuttan a piece, min.'*

sib *adj.* related to one another. *'Oh yaas, they're sib, they both hiv Moar blood in them.'*

sibble *v.* sip, keep drinking.

sidelegs *adv.* (to sit) with both legs on one side e.g in riding a horse. **sideleens, sidelins** *adv.* sideways. *move sideleens* i.e. crab fashion. **sidieweys** sideways. *'Pit hid in sidieweys.'*

sids *n.* outer husks of grain.

sile *n.* a young herring (no more than the size of one's little finger).

sillock, sillo *n.* a one year coalfish.

Silver Willie *n.* a top shell.

simman *n.* straw rope twisted and plaited.

simmet *n.* vest.

sindrie *adv.* apart. *tae tak things sindrie* to take things apart.

single *v.* thin out, *tae single neeps* to remove the surplus plants leaving *single* plants about 15 cms apart. Weeds are removed at the same time.

sinkie, sinko *n.* a small depression.

sinnie fynnie *n.* the black guillemot.

sinny-girs *n.* couch grass.

sirp *n.* wet ground. **sirpan, sypan** *adj.* soaking wet, *'Me feet wis just sirpan.'* **sirpis** a soaking wet mess.

sitten *adj.* an egg which has an embryo chicken inside it.

skaad-head *n.* the shell of the sea-urchin.

skael *v.* scatter.

skaeliment *n.* violent scattering; sudden disorder. *'He meed a right skaeliment in the supermarket when he knockit ower that pile o tins.'*

skaively, skeffly *adj.* clumsy, especially *skaively-feeted* walking with the feet out and in a clumsy fashion.

skaoowaoo *adj.* twisted, off the straight.

skarf, skarfie, skart *n.* the cormorant or the shag. **tae baet skarfs** to beat the hands against the sides of the chest to warm them in the manner of the *skarf* beating its wings to dry them.

skarr *adj.* frightened or nervous. *'A naafil skarr thing o bern.'*

skate-rumple *n.* a nickname for an inhabitant of Deerness.

skat† *n.* old land tax. **skatfa, skam-skatfa** *n.* ruin. *'His ferm's just geen tae skatfa.'* **skatfo** *adj.* **1** greedy. **2** wasteful.

skeeleen goose *n.* the sheldrake.

skeet *v.* **1** squirt or shoot out. **2** skim a stone over water so that it bounces off the surface. **3** make unkind remarks about someone. **skeeto** *n.* **1** the cuttlefish. **2** the sea anemone. **3** a squirt.

skegg *n.* the beard or awn of the bere seed. **skeggs** woody fibrous material in a peat bank.

skelder, skolder *v.* make a loud noise. **skelder, skolder, skyolder** *n.* **1** noisy talk. **2** a strong breeze. **3** the screaming of seagulls. **4** the oyster catcher. **5** *a skolder o bones* a very thin person (a rattling skeleton). *tae go doon in a skyolder* to go down with a loud crash.

skeldro *n.* **1** the oyster catcher. **2** the shelduck.

skelf *n.* **1** shelf **2** a thin piece of skin torn off. **3** a splinter of wood.

Skellat, Skellit, Skillet *n.* one of the smaller bells in St Magnus Cathedral.

skelp¹ *n.* a large extent. *a skelp o land.*

skelp², skyelp *v.* & *n.* smack with the flat of the hand.

skinniebreeks *n.* a shellfish (*mya arenaria*) so called from the appearance of its syphon.

skint *v.* hurry. '*Skint thee noo!*'

skirl *v.* make a shrill noise. **skirler** *n.* a strong gale. **skirlie** a fried mixture of meal and onions.

skirlo *n.* a small, hand made wooden propeller which turns in the wind; also *tirlo.*

skirp, skyirp, skerp *n.* a large rip in clothing. **skirpan, shirpan,**

skyirpan *adj.* especially in *skirpan clean* of cloth after it has been washed. (the word relates to the sound made by drawing the fingers along clean fibres e.g. newly washed hair).

skite *v.* slide.

skitter¹ **(the)** (vulgar) *n.* diarrhoea, esp *a dose o the skitter.* *v.* excrete diarrhoea.

skitter² *v.* & *n.* work in an unmethodical way. *tae skitter aboot.* *n.* a hurry, trying to do several things at once. *in a skitter.* **skitter-broltie** the corn bunting.

skon *n.* a cake of cow dung.

skoot¹ *v.* jut out. *n.* a jutting out.

skoot², skout *n.* **1** the razor-bill. **2** the common guillemot.

skorie¹ *n.* a young seagull. A children's rhyme runs:-
Tammy Norie
(or Nickol Gorie)
Catched a skorie
On the Peedie Sea,
He gid him a nippie
Apin the hippie
And than he let him flee.

skorie² *n.* a crowd or troop. (compare the old North Ronaldsay rhyme):-
Come oot - Green Gorey
Wi a thee skorie
An follow thoo me tae the sea.
These words were spoken by the seal wife who returned to land to collect the cow and calves she owned.

skran *n.* a morsel, *'Thir wisna wan skran left efter they hid been there.'*

skreed, skrythe, skry, skro *v.* swarm. *n.* **1** a swarm. **2** a crowd.

skreever *n.* a howling gale, literally a tearing or scratching wind.

skrek *v.* talk with a high pitched voice. *n.* a high pitched yell.

skrog *n.* a tough root or old branch found in peat.

skroo[1] *v.* stack sheaves. *n.* a stack of sheaves.

skroo[2], **skroa, skrow, skreu** *n.* fragments, *'Whin I opened the biscuits they were aal in skroo.'*

skroolt *v.* make a grating noise.

skruff[1] *n.* shaggy hair, *a skruff o hair.*

skruff[2] *n.* **1** a piece of coarse dry skin. **2** dry crust of bread.

skrullyie, skraal, skrallyo *v.* swarm, especially *skrullyan alive. 'His head wis skrullyan alive wi lice.' n.* a crowd or swarm of something, especially lice.

skry, skro see **skreed.**

skuitsie, skitsie *adj.* (of the feet etc.) sticking out.

skull *v.* throw a small flattish stone over the surface of a flat stretch of water at a low angle so that the stone bounces repeatedly before sinking. (also *skeet*).

skurt *v.* carry an object or bundle against the lower part of the body with both arms around it. *n.* the lap.

skuther, skwither, skudder *v.* **1** scrape, *'I skuthered me shins against the wall.'* **2** bounce a flat stone along the surface of a pool etc., (also *skeet* and *skull*). *n.* a gale or shower.

skyo, skeo, skio, skoo *n.* a roughly built hut of wood or stones for drying peats etc, formerly used for drying fish and flesh.

skyran *adj.* very colourful.

slaister, slester *v.* make a mess. *n.* **1** a wet mess. **2** a bungling job. **3** a careless worker. **slaisterie** *adj.* messy in the sense of wet.

slap *n.* a small field gate.

slap dab *adj.* slap dash.

slatero , slatroo, slaterworm *n.* woodlouse.

sleekid *adj.* sly.

slerp *v.* slobber *n.* lick. *a slerp o a kiss* a wet kiss. *'Gae hid a slerp o paint.'* paint it, but don't be too particular.

slide *v.p.t.* **sled** *p.p.* **slidden** slide. **slido** *n.* a patch of ice made into a slide. **slidy** *adj.* **1** slippery. **2** underhand.

slite *adj.* **1** smooth **2** level. *The snow wis slite wi the dike.*

slock *v.* **1** extinguish a fire. **2** quench a thirst.

slurk *n.* a noise made when drinking.

slygoose *n.* the shelduck, from its secretive nesting habits. (the word *goose* was applied to birds other than geese; compare **emmergoose** the great northern diver).

slykees *n.* barnacles. (also known as **kleck-geese**; it was popularly believed that barnacle geese were born from barnacles.)

sma *adj.* small. **sma breid** rolls or *cookies.* **sma drink** used negatively, *'He's no sma drink'* he's very important. **sma hunner/hunder** a hundred, as opposed to the bigger hundred of six score (see **long hunder**). **smatings** odds and ends.

smeeo hole *n.* a small opening in a henhouse to let the hens in and out, or a small opening in a dyke for sheep to pass through.

smero, smerow, smuiro *n.* **1** clover. **2** bird's foot trefoil. **3** tormentil. A clover leaf was worn in the boot on market day to prevent the wearer being cheated.

> *A muckle gold smaroo for*
> *Maroo,*
> *And May flooers for Marget*
> *and thee;*
> Harriet Campbell, *Kitty*
> *Buddoo.*

smerslin, smurslin, smirlin *n.* the sand gaper, a shell found on sandy beaches (*mya truncata*).

smiddie *n.* a smithy.

smikker *v.* smirk.

smit *v.* infect. **smitsom** *adj.* infectious.

smook *v.* (of fine snow) blow around. *n.* **1** fine powdery snow being driven around. **2** coal dust (Westray). **3** smithereens. *lyan in smook. Tae go like smook*, to go very fast.

smoor *v.* **1** (of fine powdery snow) blow, especially in a whirling fashion, *'Hid's fairly smooran ootside noo.'* **2** choke. *'He's just*

smoored wi the cowld.' **3** damp down a fire. **4** drown.

smuggle *v.* in *the Ba* to conceal the ball and move it by deception towards the goal. *n.* such a move.

smush, smoosh *n.* smoke or dust flying about. *aal in smush* completely broken up.

smuthereen, smithereen *n.* **1** a small amount (e.g. of butter on bread). **2 the smuthereens o day** faint light in the sky at dawn or twilight.

sna *n.* snow. **snawie** *adj.* snowy. **snawie-fowl** the snow bunting.

sneck *n.* a door latch.

sneer, sneeter *v. tae sneer wi the cowld* to have a bad head cold. *sneeteran wi the cowld* with nose running because of a head cold.

sneeshan, snysin *n.* the coot. (also known as the **snellie** and the **snyth**).

sneeter[1]**, snutter** *v.* giggle, especially *sneeteran and laughan.*

sneeter[2] *v.* (of new cheese) make a squeaky sound when cut.

snellie *n.* the coot.

snib *v.* **1** fasten (a door etc.) with a catch. **2** cut short. *tae snib tatties*, to break off the shoots to prevent them growing.

snicker *n.* a suppressed laugh, snigger.

snickle *n.* a twitch for a horse, a loop of rope passing round a horse's nose and tightened with a short stick. It was used to restrain an awkward animal e.g. in shoeing.

snifter *n.* **1** the beginning of a head cold. **2** a light shower. **3** hint, inkling.

snippo, snippack *n.* a snipe.

snirl *v.* **1** (of a rope) twist. **2** twist the face, especially, *tae snirl up the nose. n.* a twist.

snorrie-bone *n.* a child's toy, made by threading a bone or large button on a loop of string, spinning it round and pulling the ends of the loop to make a snoring noise.

snow *n.* snow. **snowfang** *n.* snowdrift (see **fann**) **snowflake** *n.* **1** snowflake. **2** a snowbunting.

snuid¹ *n.* **1** a knot. **2** a twist. *'Whit a snuid's in the back o that sheep.'*

snuid² *n.* a ribbon formerly used by unmarried girls for tying up their hair. The *snuid* was burned as part of the wedding ritual in a ceremony known as the *swee-een o the snuid.*

snuid³ *n.* the name formerly used by boys in Stromness for a short piece of fishing line.

snushan *adj.* snorting, expelling air noisily through the nose. *'I widna trust a snushan bull.' snushan and sleepan*, breathing heavily through the nose while sleeping.

soapie blots *n.* soapy water in which something has been washed.

sock *n.* ploughshare.

solan goose *n.* the gannet.

soldier *n.* **1** soldier. **2** a stalk of plantain, used to 'play soldiers', a game in which two children, in turn, try to knock the head off the plantain held by the other.

sole stockings *n.* stocking soles.

some *adj.* **1** some. **2** extraordinary, used in Orkney in a peculiar way, *'He's some man!', 'That's some good!.'* **somewey** *adv.* **1** somehow, *'He got the engine stert somewey or ither.'* **2** somewhere. *'He wis been somewey and gotten this bag o fish.'* **somepiece** somewhere. *'Whar's me glesses? I laid them doon somepiece here.'*

soo *n.* sow (pig). *'The soo's run across hid'* something has been spoiled or ruined e.g. a relationship. **soofish** *n.* sowfish, the wrasse. **soo shell** the truncated gaper shell. Orkney shells were given animal names by children who used them for farm games.

sooans *n.* oat flour slightly fermented. The inner husks of oats are soaked for some days then strained and the resultant paste is used for making special scones. **sooan scones** very thin pancakes made from *sooans.* **sooan sids** *sooan* husks.

sook¹ *n.* dry conditions. *'Hid's makkan a fine sook the day'* usually associated with a drying wind. **yardsook** strong breeze to dry stacks. *v.* dry **sookid fish** dried fish.

sook² *v.* strike a blow. *n.* a blow, (also **sooker**), *'He gid him a right sook on the side o the head.'*

sook[3] *v.* suck. *n.* **1** a call to a calf. **2** a call to cattle when driving them to get them to move on. **sookie** a child's comforting blanket or rag. **sook-in** a disappointment.

sookan *n.* a straw rope twisted in a single strand.

Sookener *n.* a nickname for an inhabitant of Burness parish, Sanday.

soond[1] *n.* a narrow stretch of water.

soond[2] *adj.* sound (in condition), especially as negative, *no soond* not of sound mind.

soople *n.* that part of the flail which strikes the grain. *adj.* agile, supple.

soor *adj.* sour. **tae soor cuithes** gut coalfish, split and leave for four days to sour before eating.

soorick, sooro *n.* sorrel or dock.

sooth *n.* **1** south. **2** specifically, across the Pentland Firth, especially *aff sooth*, on the Scottish mainland or in England. **Sooth Country** originally the land across the Pentland Firth (as in Dennison's story) now used only as *adj.* in *Sooth Country folk*, particularly English people.

sot *adv.* a form of *so* used by children in an argument e.g. Child A: '*Dis not*', Child B: '*Dis sot.*' '*Ah'm no faerd!*' '*Thoo er sot!*'

sowder *v. & n.* solder.

spaek *v.p.t.* **spak** *p.p.* **spocken** speak. **spaekan proper** attempting to speak a standard English but 'showing off.' **tae spaek in by** to call in for a chat. **caase a**

speakeen do something to become a subject of gossip. '*Dinno deu that for hid might caase a spaekeen.*'

spaekalation *n.* a subject for gossip. '*Whit a spaekalation hid wid be if we hid tae sell the ferm.*

spang *n.* a long stride.

spare *v.* spare. '*If we're spared*', God willing. '*We'll go tae the toon the morn if we're spared.*'

speeder *n.* spider.

speer *v.* enquire, ask. '*Yi'll hae tae speer the bung o the tar barrel*' a retort to an impertinent question.

spell, speel *v.* take a turn at work, '*Ah'll spell yi noo.*' *n.* **1** spell of time. **2** a period of hard work. **3** a splinter of wood.

spew *v.* spew. **speweens** *n.* vomit, '*The bairn's claes wis just covered wi speweens.*'

spick *n.* fat, especially pork fat.

spin *v.* (of a cat) purr, preserved in the old rhyme:-
Cat i the mill door, spinnan, spinnan
By cam a peerie moose, rinnan, rinnan
Whit's that thoo're spinnan, me lady, me lady?
Cotton breeks tae me son,
Fause thief - Ah'll hae thee.

spleet-new *adj.* brand new.

splushnie *n.* a catapult.

spoag *n.* spoke of a wheel.

spoot *n.* **1** spout. **2** razor fish. **3** a rain gutter under the eaves of a house. **4** lemonade. **spoot whale** a porpoise. **spoot ebb** '*Thir should be a good spoot-ebb the* *night'*, in the spring of the year the sea ebbs far out and allows *spoots* to be caught. **spoot girse** angelica, cow parsley, used by young boys for making water squirts. **spootricks, splutter** butter softened in the mouth before it is applied to bread. (An old story known throughout Orkney tells of the herdie boy taking shelter in a house who was offered a biscuit and butter by an old lady. She gave him the choice of *toomspread* or *spootricks*. He did not know what *spootricks* was but looking at her dirty hands he decided that this method could not be worse than butter spread by her thumb. He must have regretted his decision!)

spraagle *v.* sprawl, flounder about.

spret *v.* **1** jump quickly, *'Whit a fleg I got whin this man spret oot o the ditch.'* **2** burst, especially of a seam, *'Mercy Ah'm spret the seam o me coat.'* *n.* a jump.

sprig *n.* a little nail used in cobblery.

spring *v.* **1** spring. **2** strain. *'Watch and no spring theesael wi liftan that weight.'* **springan** in a state of agitation to go to the toilet, *'Ah'm just springan.'* *n.* Spring. *in the Spring o the 'ear,* in Springtime. (This is the only season referred to in this way).

sproll *n.* a curved rod made of stout wire on the end of a fishing line to which two hooks are attached by means of two pieces of *snuid*.

sprug, spyug *n.* sparrow.

spuin *n.* spoon. **spuin cubbie** a small container made of straw for holding spoons.

spulyie *n.* driftwood.

spunk, sprunk *n.* a spark of fire. **spunkie** *n.* a small torch. **spunkies** distant flashes of lightning with no sound of thunder (also known as **weather blinks**).

spurrie *n.* **1** an earwig. **2** any fast moving insect.

spurrie-girse *n.* cow parsnip.

square tree *n.* a game played in Sanday similar to pulling the **sweerie stick** but the stick was held aloft and the challenger was required to twist the stick and touch one end on the ground.

stab *n.* a fencing post.

stael *v.p.t.* **stelt** *p.p.* **stelt** (formerly *stown*) steal.

staff *n.* **1** a staff. **2** a walking stick. (When Lord Kitchener and his staff were lost off Birsay in World War I, an old gentleman said he could understand the concern about the loss of this great man but he did not know why such a fuss was being made about the loss of his walking stick!)

staig *n.* stallion, male horse kept for breeding.

stair exe *n.* North Ronaldsay sheepmark.

stane, steen, ston *n.* a stone. *'He's liftan a stone tae brak his ain head wi'*, what he is doing will ruin him. **staneputter, steenie-pouter** the turnstone. **steenie-picker** the sand-piper.

stap *v.* cram, pack in firmly, *'Stap hid aal in the barrel beuy'* Sometimes used jocularly of food, *'Stap hid in beuy.'* **stappit** *adj.* replete, stuffed.

starn *n.* stern of a boat.

steb only in compounded forms *steb-mither, steb-sister* etc., step-mother, step-sister.

steck *v.* 1 walk determinedly, *'Whar ar thoo steckan tae the day?'* 2 tether. *'Gyung and steck the coo on new girse.'* *n.* a stake.

steedeen *n.* a group of farm buildings, *the steedeen o Binscarth.*

steen-biter *n.* the lump sucker fish.

steer , steero *n.* confusion. *'Whit a steero we were in whin the visitors cam.'*

steethe *n.* the foundation of a haystack etc.

stick *v.* stick. **stick in** persevere, apply oneself. *'Stick in noo!'* Eat up! a phrase used at table. **stickid** *adj.* (of a person, animal, the wind etc) determined, perverse. *'That's a stickid thing o coo that.'* **stickid stoor** blinding snow which sticks to clothing. **stickie-willie** goosegrass. **tae tak the stick** to refuse to move (e.g. of an animal).

stiggie *n.* a starling.

stiggle *n.* poor thin crop, poor straw.

still-stand *adv.* stand-still.

stilt *n.* an elevated foundation for a corn stack (Birsay).

stime¹ *n.* 1 a tiny amount 2 glimmer of light. *'I couldna see a stime'* I could see nothing.

stime² *v.* stare.

stingie-bee *n.* a wild bee.

stinkie-buil *n.* wheatear.

stirk, strik *n.* a young ox.

stirleen *n.* 1 a starling. 2 nickname for a Kirkwall person. **stirleen snow** stormy, snowy weather in May when starlings congregate.

stivven *v.* stiffen, congeal. *'A'm just stivvnan wi the cowld.'* I'm freezing cold.

stob *n.* remains of a feather on a plucked hen. **stobbie** *adj.* prickly.

stock duck *n.* the mallard. **stock-whaup** the curlew. **stock, lock and barrel** an example of many transposed phrases in the dialect.

stockeen *n.* stocking. **stockeen feet** with no shoes on. *'He wis gan aboot in his stockeen feet.'*

stomach *n.* 1 stomach. 2 appetite, *'Ah'm fairly lost me stomach'* I have completely lost my appetite. **stomachless** having no appetite.

stone-chat *n.* a wheatear.

stoo, styoo *v.* cut off, especially of hair. *n.* a sheep's mark, the tip of the ear clipped off. **stoo and bits** a sheepmark. **stooed hemlin** half the ear cut off at a slant. **stooed rip** a slit made in the ear after the point has been cut off.

stook¹ *n.* a sheepmark.

stook² *n.* a group of six sheaves set up in a field to dry. *v.* set up sheaves. **stookie Sunday** the Sunday when the greatest number of stooks were to be seen in the fields. *stand like a stookie* stand as if unable to move.

stoond *n.* **1** a mood or whim. **2** a stab of pain. **stoondie** *adj.* moody.

stoop, stow *exclam.* **1** Be quiet! **2** You don't mean it! used as a reaction to an unbelievable piece of news.

stoor *v.* move quickly. *'He fairly stoored doon the road.'* *n.* dust.

Stoorworm (The) *n.* a sea-monster of Orkney folk-lore.

stoot *adj.* stout.

stop *v.* **1** stop. **2** live, dwell, *'We stoppid in a caravan till the roof wis mended.'*

storm-finch *n.* the stormy petrel.

stott[1] *v.* bounce, reel about because of tiredness or drunkeness. *'He wis so drunk he wis just stottan along the street.'*

stott[2] *n.* a bullock.

strae *n.* straw. *'Yi canna draa a strae across his baird the day'* He is in no mood for teasing. **strae/straa backid stuil** the correct name for an Orkney chair.

straik *v.* **1** stroke. **2** stretch. *n.* a stroke.

stram *n.* a state of excitement or anxiety, a hurry, *'He wis in a stram tae feeneesh the wark and get awey tae the toon.'*

straps *n.* **1** straps. **2** braces.

stravaig *v.* wander about.

streen (the) *n.* yesterday evening.

streyt *ad.* straight.

strick[1] *v.p.t.* **strack** *p.p.* **stricken, strucken** strike. **a strucken oor** a whole hour by the clock, a long boring time.

strick[2] *n.* stirk.

stridelegs, stridielegs *adv.* with legs apart, *tae sit stridelegs on a horse.*

strill *n.* the starling.

string *n.* a strong current flowing through a narrow strip of water. **The String** is the channel between Shapinsay and The Mainland).

strip *n.* **1** a strip. **2** a stripe. **strippid** striped.

stripe *v.* milk a cow, get the last drops.

stroop *n.* the spout of a kettle or teapot.

stuil *n.* a chair, especially *straabackid stuil*, the correct name for the Orkney chair.

sturt *n.* movement, *No muckle sturt there yet. The lum's no even reekan.'* **sturtsome** *adj.* active.

styman *adj.* very drunk and walking as if blind. *'He wis just styman.'*

suck[1] *n.* **1** a mess, a quagmire **2** a dirty person. **suckie** *adj.* dirty.

suck[2] *n.* straw or withered grass in a hen's nest in particular but also under an animal.

sucken *adj.* **1** sunk. *'His eyes wir just sucken in his head.'* **2** marshy, especially *sucken hole* used to describe the situation of a farm etc.

sugg *n.* a piece of hardened skin on the hands.

suit *v.* suit. *'You suit that colour'*, That colour suits you.

summer-whaap *n.* the whimbrel, also known as the **May bird**.

sun-sitten *adj.* of eggs, addled and spoiled by the heat of the sun.

supper *n.* supper. *v.* feed cattle or horses at night, '*Ah'll come in when Ah'm suppered the horse.*'

swack *adj.* 1 (of a person) fit or agile. 2 (of an animal) in good condition.

swadge *v.* sit down and relax after a meal. *n.* rest after eating.

swall *v. & n.* swell.

swander *v. & n.* lurch.

swap *n.* a gust of wind. *v.* gust **swappan for aaks** catching auks by sweeping a special net over the cliff face.

swarbie, swarfarro, swartback *n.* the black backed gull. (also known as **ritto**).

swarfish *n.* the spotted blenny.

swash *n.* a quantity of liquid, '*Gae me a swash o tea.*' '*A great swash o water cam ower the side.*'

swee *v.* 1 smart (e.g. of a hurt finger), especially from a burn. 2 to burn, of a crop on shallow soil. 3 singe feather remains on a plucked hen etc. **the swee-een o the snuid** see **snuid**.

sweenkle, swink *v.* gurgle. When the stomach is full of liquid it is said to *sweenkle*.

sweerie-stick, swera-tree *n.* a stick used in an old game. This trial of strength was called *pullan the sweerie-stick*. The contestants sat on the floor facing each other with their feet against their partner's feet and pulled with both hands at a stick held at right angles to their arms.

sweet-milk *n.* fresh milk as distinct from sour milk.

swick *v.* swindle. *n.* 1 a swindle. 2 a swindler.

swilkie, swelchie *n.* a whirlpool. A famous whirlpool in the Pentland Firth is known as *The Swilkie*.

swill *v.* swill. *n.* a quick wash, '*Gae yir face a swill.*'

swilter, swiller, switter *v.* shake and splash (e.g. of water in a bucket).

swine-fish *n.* the wolf fish.

swirdy, swirdo, swirdack *n.* 1 the blenny. 2 a poor thin cod.

switter *v.* be in a flurry.

sye[1] *n.* scythe.

sye[2] *v.* strain or filter (e.g. milk or newly boiled potatoes) '*Mercy Ah'm forgotten tae sye the tatties and they're aal in a slester.*' **syer** *n.* 1 a strainer for milk. 2 a grid covering a drain.

syes, syves *n.* chives.

sype *v.* drain dry.

synsin *n.* the coot.

T

taas (the) *n.* a leather belt formerly used by teachers to punish children.

tacketie buits *n.* hobnail boots.

tae¹ *prep.* **1** to. **2** for, '*Go and git some nails tae me.*' '*Ah'll boil a egg tae his tea.*' '*Ah'm knittan a jersey tae Freddy.*' '*He works tae Swanbister.*'

tae² *n.* toe.

taebeck *n.* the call of the red grouse.

taek *n.* tack (of a ship).

tagsie *adj.* untidy.

tail *n.* **1** tail. **2** a tail shaped piece of land. *v.* cut the tail off, especially turnips, '*We tailed twa three dreel o neeps afore denner.*' **tail girdeen** that part of a horse's harness which goes under the tail. **tail puddeen** a very fatty type of mealy pudding used to counteract the effect of alcohol. The fiddler who played at a wedding feast was traditionally met at the yard slap (gate) and had to eat a *tail puddeen* to ensure that he remained sober for a reasonable period of time. **tail sweepers** the last couple at the end of a wedding procession who, with besoms, removed the evidence of the party and prevented evil spirits following in their train. This couple were doomed to remain unmarried for a year. **Taily Day, Taileen Day** the second day of April. It was common throughout Orkney until fairly recently to pin a *tail* secretly on someone as a prank.

taing, teeng *n.* a point of land; common in placenames.

tak *v.p.t.* **tuk, tuik** *p.p.* **taen, tin, teen**. take. '*The frost's taen the air*' the air is very cold. **tak at** get on with it; do the other thing; lump it. '*If tho disno like hid, thoo can just tak at.*' **tae be taen** to die; in olden days it was taboo to use the name of someone who had recently died '*Him (or her) thit was taen*' was used instead. **tae tak oot 1** to take peats from the person cutting them and to set them on the bank. **2** (of weather) to improve. **tae tak paece** to settle down, '*I wish that bairn wid tak paece.*' **tae tak tae** to start to. '*He tuk tae the laugheen.*' He started to laugh. **tae tak tae the eyes** start to cry. **tae tak up** of a fire to begin to burn more strongly.

Tammie *n.* Tommy. **Tammie-Noddie 1** the puffin. **2** sleep in the eye. (also known as **Henry Noddie**). **Tammie-Norrie 1** the puffin. **2** the sea-shell, fool's cap. **Tammie o Tirlybraes** a legendary evil man whose name was invoked to scare naughty children. **Tammie reekie** a cabbage stalk hollowed out filled with tar and set alight. (also known as a **Smoky Tom**.)

70

tang *n.* seaweed; *tang* grows above the low-water mark, *ware* below. **tang cowes** seaweed fronds. **Tangie** a mythical sea spirit surrounded by a fire glow of phosphorescence. **tangie** a seal, because of its association with *tang*. **tang-sparrow** the rock pipit. **tangie-spur** a small kind of seal. **tang-whaup** the whimbrel. **tang whaeser, tangie-whaesie** a small seal.

tanny *adj.* tawny, especially *tanny skinned*, dark skinned.

tap *n.* top. **the tap o the day** noon. **tapo, tappie-whaesie** the shag, so called from the tuft on its head. **tapmost** highest.

tappie *adj.* silly.

tarf *adj.* **1** rancid. **2** rough, fierce, *'Beuy, that's gey tarf, the wey thoo're playan wi the bairn.'*

tarrie fingered *adj.* inclined to steal.

tarpalyin *n.* tarpaulin.

tarrock *n.* a tern or similar type of bird.

taste *n.* taste, *'They never askid me whether I hid taste or smell'* They offered me nothing to eat. **tasteless, taseless** *adj.* **1** tasteless. **2** sad, disappointing, *'Sheu haed a kind o taseless homecomeen, coman home tae a funeral.'* (Westray).

tattie, tatta *n.* potato. **tattie-bogle** a scare-crow. **tattie-chapper** potato masher. **tattie-shaa** potato foliage.

tattle *v.* handle with dirty fingers, *'Luk at me book, hid's aal tattled.'*

taupie-goat *n.* a fool.

tear and wear wear and tear.

teddrie-tail *n.* an earwig.

teebro, teedburn, teedburrow, tidburn, tidbirn, tidbrim *n.* heat shimmer which appears over the hills on a warm summer's day:- *When yi see the teebro's flyan Hid's a sign the grund is dryan.*

teefie, teefie bit *exclam.* devil-a-bit.

teeick, teeo, teewhuppo *n.* lapwing. **teeick snow** snow which falls in March.

teengs *n.* tongs.

teenk-tank *n.* the sound of milk being squirted from the cow's udder into a pail. An old riddle runs, *'Teenk-tank under a bank, ten aboot fower'* the answer is 'a cow being milked.' cf. **pink-peenk.**

teet *v. & n.* peep.

teeteen, teetan *n.* the meadow pipit.

teeter *v.* laugh in a secretive manner.

teeth *n.* **1** teeth. **2** a tooth, *'Ah'm been tae the dentist and hin me teeth oot,'* an old lady remarked, *'All of them?!'* the visitor asked in surprise. *'No, just the wan,'* was the confusing reply! **teethache, tuithache** toothache. **teethbrush** a toothbrush. *'Feth I hiv aal me back teeth up'* I wasn't born yesterday.

teewallop-teeweep *n.* the call of the lapwing.

tefferie, tefterie *adj.* fussy, having a poor appetite.

tell *v.p.t.* **telled, tellt** *p.p.* **tellt** tell. **tae tell apin** to tell on, *'I wisna supposed tae go ootside bit the postman tellt apin me.'* *n.* word, news. *'Wir never heard tell o him since.'*

tell-pie, tale-pie *n.* a tell-tale:-
Tell-pie, tell pie sittan on the midden,
Pickan ap hen dirt when he wisno bidden.'

tepp *v.* dam water. **teppin** *n.* a dam.

Term Day the day on which a farm labourer's contract began or ended, corresponding to English Quarter Days. The Term Days were Candlemas (2 Feb), Whitsunday (15 May), Lammas (1 Aug) and Martinmas (11 Nov).

Terran *n.* a mythical monster in Orkney folklore who annually battled in Springtime with the spirit the *Mither o the Sea* in a duel known as the *vore tullye* and who was silenced until Autumn when he resumed battle in the *gore vellye*. In this encounter he emerged victor and ruled the seas for the winter months.

terry hatters *n.* a children's playground game played at Firth School similar to *cops and robbers.*

teu *prep.* to. *adv.* also. **teu-name** a nickname, usually a parish nickname; see **Merry Dancers** as an example.

thaft, taft *n.* a seat in rowing boat, a thwart.

than *conj.* then. *'He wis seen ahint the byre an than he gid tae the shore an that wis the last time he wis seen.'* **thanadays** *in those days.*

that *pron.* that, those. **that wans** those. The plural form *those* is not used. *'Gae me that wans.'*

the *def. art.* **1** used instead of a possessive pronoun eg *the wife* instead of *my wife.* **2** used frequently where English would miss it out e.g. *'Ah'm gan tae the kirk'*, *'The bairns are awey tae the school'*, *'John's for the toon'*, *'He tuk tae the laugheen'* (He started to laugh). **3** used derogatorily instead of a possessive, *'He wis standan there, the fag in the mooth'*, *'The mither o him wis nivver home.'* **4** as in 2, the definite article is frequently used before professions e.g. *'He works at the joiner wark'*, *'He wrowt at the plumber wark a whilie.'* **5** *the day, the morn, the night*, today, tomorrow, tonight.

thee[1] *pron. acc. dat. voc. of* thoo. *'I saa thee yesterday.'* *'Ah'll gae thee some.'* *'Thee tak/Tak thee the shovel.'* Also used reflexively. *'Sit thee doon.'*

thee[2] *poss. pron. sing* your. *'Come thee wiz.'*

them *pron.* them. **them wans** sometimes used as accusative/dative plural of *that. Those* is never used.

thight *adj.* **1** tight. **2** tight-lipped.

thing, ting *n.* thing. **peerie ting, peedie ting, pee ting** some small living thing, especially a child. **bit-a-ting** used sentimentally of a small child *'The bairn's fa'n and cut hidsael, the bit-a-ting.'*

thingimur *n.* thingamagig.

think, tink *v.p.t.* **thowt** *p.p.* **thowt** think *tae think long for* to long for. *tae think tae* to have an opinion of *'Whit are yi thinkan tae this weather?'*

thir[1] *pron.+v.* they are.

thir[2] *pron.+v.* there are, there is.

this *pron.* this, these. **this wans** these. (cf. **that**).

thistlecock *n.* corn-bunting.

thole *v.* endure, put up with, suffer.

thoo *pron. nom. sing.* you. *'Thoo kens whit hid's like wi a hooseful o folk.'*

thornie-skate *n.* the skate (fish), so called because of the thorns on its back.

thraa,traa *v.* twist, especially to *thraa the neck* the traditional method of killing a hen. **in a thraa/traa** in a knot. **thraan** awkward, cross-grained.

thraep, traep *v.* argue persistently, insist, usually used with *'doon the throt.'* *'He was aye thraepan doon wir throts hoo muckle fish he hid catched in his younger days.'*

thrang, trang *adj.* busy.

thrapple, trapple *v.* choke *'Mercy he nearly thrappled me.'* *n.* throat, especially *tae weet the thrapple'* to have a drink.

thrift, trift *n.* **1** thrift. **2** energy *'He didna hiv the thrift tae get aff his erse and help his owld mither.'*

thuddie *adj.* (of the wind) gusty.

thunderer *n.* a bull roarer.

tide-lump *n.* rough patch of sea caused by current and wind running against each other.

tift *v.* **1** (of an injured finger etc.) throb. **2** (of bones) ache.

tig *n.* a children's game known elsewhere as 'catch.' **tig-tag, teeg-tag** *n.* suspense. **had him in teeg-tag** hold him in suspense; keep him guessing.

tilter, tilder, toolter *v.* sway or totter. **tilterie, toolterie, tuiltrie** *adj.* **1** tottering, unstable. **2** (of clothes) shabby.

timmers *n.* ribs of a boat.

tink see **think**.

tinkler *n.* a tinker. **tink, tinkie** disrespectful forms of 'tinkler.' **tinkie's punishment** a game played by children. It consisted of grasping the four fingers of a partner and rubbing the finger tips firmly and quickly with the knuckles.

tinnie *n.* a tin mug. *'Sheu's as mean as tea in a tinnie.'* Too mean to use a cup for the tea!

tirl *v.* **1** turn. **2** upset by turning. **3** poke in the earth. *n.* **1** the wheel of the old click mill. **2** a spell of bad weather *'The Beltane tirls.'*

tirlo[1]**, tirlick** a small windwill made for a child. **the Tirlos, Tirlies** the wind generators on Burgar Hill.

tirlo², **tirlack** a wrestling game in which a wrestler attempts to throw his opponent. **tirler** fastening on a door.

tirrie, tirrie-wirrie *adj.* cross, petulant, peevish.

tirso *n.* 1 the dock. 2 marsh ragwort, especially the dried stem. *Sheu's nither a tirso nor a dochan*; fish aren't taking the bait.

tise, tice *v.* persuade, coax.

tishalago *n.* coltsfoot.

tisso *n.* a kiss, used by a mother to a child.

t'ither *pron.* **the t'ither,** the other, e.g. if you have four blocks of wood and you want to place them in two groups you would *'pit the wan wi the wan and the t'ither wi the t'ither.'*

tizzan *adj.* crying, especially *tizzan and greetan.*

toddo's grund *n.* in a children's game, a sanctuary.

to-fa, teu-fa, teu-fo, tufal, tuffer *n.* a small addition to a house, a lean-to.

toin *v,* shrivel, dry up.

tongue *n.* 1 tongue. 2 a tongue-shaped mark on a sheep's ear. 3 a *tongue* of land. **Tongue-noo!** Be quiet! **Had yir tongue!** 1 Be quiet! 2 You don't mean it! (a reaction to a piece of unbelievable news).'*He wis aye tongue afore teeth'* he spoke without thinking. **stappid tae the tongue root** absolutely full up. **tongue tae the erse like a trump** extremely talkative, literally having a tongue stretching down to the backside like a Jew's harp.

too, tuo, tuack *n.* 1 a tuft of grass. 2 a little knoll (a landscape feature in Sanday is called the *three toos.*).

took, tug *n.* a swig out of a bottle.

toom *n.* thumb. **toomspread** (of butter) spread with the thumb.

toon *n.* town. **the toon** *gaan tae the toon* going to either Kirkwall or Stromness whichever is one's normal service centre.

toorie *n.* 1 a bobble on a bonnet. 2 knitted hat with a bobble on it.

toot *n.* the backside, especially when talking to a child.

torno *n.* a kind of skate, so called from the *spikes* or *thorns* on its back.

tow *n.* tow. **fa in tow wi** meet by chance.

tow-lowseen *n.* a thaw.

trachle *n.* a difficulty, bother.

tramp *v.* 1 tramp. 2 wash blankets by treading on them in a large tub; *trampan blankets* was at one time an annual ritual. 3 move quickly *'He wis fairly trampan'* He was moving quickly by car, motor-cycle, etc.

trattle-bogie *n.* chatter-box.

trim *v.* repair. (*trim* also has this meaning in English though *repair* would invariably be used today).

trimse *v.* move impatiently off one leg on to another like a child needing to go to the toilet. **trimso** *n. in a trimso, in his trims* in an agitated state. *in trimso* (of a cow) ready to give birth.

trindlie, trinluie *adj.* thin, flimsy. *trindlie-leggid* spindly legged.

trinlicks, trinley pins an old game in which wooden replicas of farm animals etc (each with a different value) had to be removed carefully from a heap without disturbing the others.

Tring *n.* a Stronsay goblin.

trink, trinkie *n.* a small ditch or cleft.

trip-trap-truiskie *n.* the game of *noughts and crosses.* In Harray the winner called *'Trip-trap-trullyo!'* on winning a game of noughts and crosses.

troot *n.* a trout. *plural* **troots.** *tae go tae the troots* to go angling. **trootie hoose** a trout trap built beside a burn e.g. at Tormiston Farm Stenness or Hybreck in Harray. *tae laek like a trootie hoose* used of a badly built dwelling.

trot, throt *n.* throat.

trow *n.* a troll. In Ork legend there were *hill-trows* and *sea-trows.* *Trow* came to be synonymous with the devil which was known as DROW. **trow tak thee** a curse. **trow glove** sea sponge, also known as Dead Man's Fingers.

trowie *n.* a troll. **trowie, trullie** *adj.* **1** sickly or ailing. **2** of poor quality. *'That's trowie things o coorteens - thir aal fa'an tae pieces wi the sun.'* **trowie-like** having the appearance of being ill. **trowie-girse, trowie-glove** the foxglove. **trowie-spindle** mare's tail (grass).

trumfs, truffs *n.* (in card games) trumps.

trump *n.* a Jew's harp.

tuction *n.* rough treatment, *'Beuy that owld bike's hin some tuction.'* **tae mak tuction** to stir up trouble.

tuilter, taulter *v.* drag behind.

tuim, toom *v.* **1** pour. **2** empty. **3** rain heavily. *adj.* **1** empty **2** hungry.

tuink *n.* a thump or crack, the sound of something heavy falling.

tuinty *adj.* tasteless, colourless. *'Sheu haed on sic a tuinty frock.'*

tulfer, tolfer *n.* a floor-board in a boat.

tullie *n.* a large kind of knife with blade fixed in the shaft.

tullimentan *adj.* (of stars) sparkling.

tumal†, toomal, tumail, tumult *n.* a field. Specifically the home field which was not part of the run-rig system. It always belonged to the adjacent dwelling as opposed to **townsland**; now only in placenames apart from the compound **hen-toomal.**

tummle *v.* tumble. **tumlan Tammie** an old horse-drawn hay rake characterised by its 'tumbling' motion.

tune *n.* **1** tune. **2** mood *'He's in poor tune the day.'*

turkey *n.* turkey. *'No more sense than a sookan turkey'*, very stupid.

turn *n.* **1** turn. **2** manner, *'He his a fine turn wi him'* He is obliging and amiable. **3** *'The days is on the turn'* daylight is lengthening. **4** *'He never does a hand's turn'*

He is extremely lazy. **tae deu the turn** to suffice. *'Hid's no muckle o a chair bit hid'll deu the turn.'* **turn ower** *v.* mention, *'Never turn hid'* Don't mention it to anyone. **turned doon** applied to the loser in the game of *square tree.*

tusk *n.* the blue catfish.

tusker, tushtar, toyster *n.* a peat cutting tool.

twa *num.* **1** two. **2** a few, *'Ah'll gae thee twa eggs tae tak home wi thee tae thee tea.'* **twa-three, twartree** a few.

twal *num.* twelve. **twal-cup** a cup of tea at 12 o'clock. **a twal-munt** a year, twelve months.

twang *n.* a thong used for tying a *'rivlin.'*

twart-back, twat-back *n.* **1** cross-beam in a roof. **2** a perch for hens.

twartleens *adv.* crosswise.

twartie *adj.* bad tempered, disagreeable.

tweeg *v.* pull.

tweesto *n.* two strands of wool twisted together.

twelp *v.* (of a lapwing) cry, *teeicks twelpan oot apae the brecks.*

twilt *n.* quilt.

twirnie, twirnie-faced *adj.* cross, awkward.

tyal *n.* a fastening.

tyned *adj.* lost, given up. *'Ach, he's tyned fancy on yin lass noo.'*

tyno *n.* a rod or wire used for hanging fish on to dry near the fire.

tyst, tystie, teistie *n.* the black guillemot.

U

ubbie see **oobie**.

udal, uthell, odal *adj*. having no feudal superior, especially *udal tenure*. **udaller** *n*. one who owns udal land.

uddie *adj*. small or insignificant. *peedie uddie, peerie-uddie* very small. *peedie-uddie-nert* very tiny amount. **udmal, odmal** very small.

ugg only in *ugg-bone* the bone behind the gills of a fish. Also known as the **ploo bone** since this bone in the cod can be carved into a little toy plough.

uiko, uikie, yuiko *n*. a small fish, the bull-head or fatherlasher. *as saat as the sea-uikie* very salty.

uim¹ *n*. a hot atmosphere. *'My whit a uim in here.'*

uim² *adj*. mad, especially of a bull or a cock. Applied metaphorically to people, *'He gid clean uim when the bairn didna deu whit hid was tellt.'*

uimest, aumest, aumestmist *adj*. uppermost, top.

uind, uin *n*. **1** a bad smell **2** the smell of mildew. **uinie** *adj*. mildewed smell. *'Whit a uinie smell wi this cloot.'*

uivigar *n*. **1** a sea urchin. **2** an ill-thriving animal. **3** untidiness, especially of the hair, *'Whit a uivigar thoo're in bairn!'* said to a young girl with long hair after she had been out in the wind.

undeeman *adj*. impossible to guess, vast, *'Hid wus undeeman the pit-props they fand at the banks.'*

unfaandoon *adj*. in a state of imminent collapse. *'That owld hoose is just unfaandoon.'*

unfaansindrie *adj*. (of a piece of equipment etc.) in a disintegrated condition.

unkan *adj*. strange, unknown. **unkans, unkas** *n*. news. *'His thoo any unkans the day?'*

unless *conj*. unless. *prep*. apart from. *'Thir wir fower folk there unless me.'*

Up-the-Gates that part of Kirkwall to the south of the Watergate, originally known as *The Laverock*. **Uppie** in the traditional *Ba* game in Kirkwall, someone born to the south of the cathedral.

upmak *n*. compensation, subsidy.

upsides (wi) *prep*. **1** attaining a certain level, standard, *'Ah'm upsides wi me wark noo'* I'm up to date. **2** equal. *'Ah'm upsides wi him noo.'*

uptail *v*. run away, turn tail. **uptail-doon** upside down.

uptak *n*. an improvement in the weather. (also **oot tak**.)

urgo bits *n*. residue in tea or ale.

77

urisland, ure† *n.* an old term for a unit of land valued at an *eyrir* that is an ounce of silver.

urm *n.* small useless potatoes, etc.

urrie, yurrie *n.* a cow's udder.

urter *n.* bare pasture, *'Eeneen's urter is morneen's fother.'* What's not worth anything at night, when you are not hungry, is quite attractive to eat in the morning when you are!

V

vaig *v.* wander about aimlessly

van *n.* **1** van. **2** travelling grocery van also known as the **motor van** or, earlier, **horse van**. **vanman** the driver of the grocery van who in the first half of this century and the latter part of the last century played a vital part in the economy of the islands not only by selling goods but also in buying farm produce, especially eggs. In the early part of this century they also bought wild birds' eggs; on one occasion a customer sold to the vanman twenty-one dozen lapwing eggs collected on the Rendall Moss.

vandit *adj.* **1** (of a cow) having stripes on the side. **2** used e.g. of a garment which has been badly dyed. **3** of a piece of knitting made from a yarn spun from more than one shade or colour.

varbo *n.* a small tumour on an animal's hide caused by the larva of the gad-fly. Also known as *aikel*.

varden *n.* a companion spirit in the shape of an animal which accompanied the individual everywhere and moaned dismally if he was about to die.

vathan-cuithe, vaan cuithe *n.* a three year old coalfish.

veegal, veekalty, veekny, veetel, veetny, vicany *n.* balance, order, only in the phrase *oot o veegal* etc. '*This holiday is pitten the week clean oot o veekalty for me.*' '*The car's oot o veekalty again.*'

veerie-orums see **eerie-orms.**

veet *n.* pronunciation of *vet*, veterinary surgeon.

veetrit *adj.* full of hatred, contemptuous, '*Ah'm nivver felt so veetrit towards anybody in me life!*'

veeze *v.* grip, seize, grab '*Veeze a had o yin rope.*'

vennel *n.* a lane. *The Vennel* was the old name for what is now St Magnus Lane in Kirkwall.

vexed *adj.* sorry. '*Ah'm that vexed I dinno hiv a sweetie tae the bairns.*'

vikkened *adj.* sturdy, well developed, '*Yin's a weel vikkened bairn.*'

vildro, vildroo, vilyero, villyero *adv.* in the phrase; *tae go vildro* to go wrong, to go to ruin, to be scattered.

voar *n.* springtime.

voe *n.* a bay or inlet of the sea, now only in placenames as in *Ronsvoe* now St Margaret's Hope Bay.

volder, voldro see **volo.**

vole-grunn *adj.* used of old earthen dividing walls or balks, known as *vole-grunn dykes.*

volo, vole-moose, volder, voldro *n.* the Orkney vole.

W

wa *n.* wall. **wa heid** the top of the wall. In the olden days, a celebration was held when a new building reached *wa heid height.* **tae stand tae the wa** (of a door) to be wide open, '*The door wis standan tae the wa.*'

waal, wael *n.* a well.

waar *adj.* worse, '*Ah'm feelan waar the day.*' '*He's tin a waar wey*' He has taken a turn for the worse. '*He's gaan bi the waar*' He's getting worse. *waar o the wear* not in good condition, '*Me gansey's the waar o the wear.*'

wabbit, wappid *adj.* tired.

wad[1] *v.* would have. '*I wad comed if hid hid been a bonny night.*' I would have come.

wad[2] *v.* wade.

waddeen *n.* wedding. **waddeen walk** in the olden days the wedding company walked to the manse for the marriage ceremony and the party was led by a fiddler followed by people sweeping the path.

waddie *n.* a ford.

wade *n.* mastitis in cattle or sheep.

wadmell† *n.* old name for home-woven cloth.

wae, we *pron.* we.

wael (oot) *v.* select, separate e.g. small potatoes from large ones or little peats from the larger peats.

waffle *v.* **1** twist, used especially of wind and rain beating down growing crop. **2** flutter in the wind. **wafflie** *adj.* shaking. *a poor wafflie buddy.*

waft, waff, wach *n.* **1** a hint of a (generally unpleasant) smell. **2** a signal. Before the days of the telephone, people used signals to communicate at a distance e.g. a sheet might be displayed in a prominent position or a *cubbie* placed on top of a high pole, such signals having a pre-determined meaning. (see **reekie brae** for another instance).

wag *n.* wag. *tae tak the wag o* to make a fool of. **wag-at-the-wa** a clock with the pendulum suspended below the body, also known as a Dutch clock.

wakkerif *adj.* sleepless, easily wakened.

wakkid *adj.* matted, shrunk, especially of a woollen garment, '*Me jersey's all wakkid under the airms.*'

Wallawa *n.* the devil.

wallie *adj.* **1** huge. **2** substantial. **Wallieman** the devil.

Walter Red, Warty Red, Wattie Reid *n.* a hobgoblin in Sandwick folklore. This name is attached to holes and depressions in the Orkney landscape e.g. 1 on the

Brough of Birsay. **2** the dip to the south of Leeon Hill in Firth and known as Stenady.

wand *n.* **1** wand. **2** a bamboo rod used for fishing cuithes. *'He laid aal his wands in the watter'* he tried his hardest.

want *v.* **1** want. *tae want home* to want to go home. **2** lack, *'A man came intae the shop wantan a leg'* caused much amusement because of its ambiguity! *n.* a lack, defect, particularly a mental defect, *'He his a kinda want aboot him.'* **wantan** *adj.* mentally defective.

wap *v.p.t.* **wappid 1** turn, e.g. the cranking handle of an old car. **2** throw or to strike with a blow, *'He wappid hid doon.'* **3** toss the arms about in walking, *'There he goes wappan along the road.'* *n.* **1** a cranking handle for an engine. **2** commotion. *'Whit a wap's in the duck hoose, there must be a rat among them.'*

ware, waar *n.* seaweed growing below the low water mark (*tang* grows above), *'The ware time is a sair time'*, an old saying meaning that it was a laborious job to manure the land with seaweed in Spring time. **ware brak** seaweed breaking loose and driving ashore in the spring and autumn. **ware cowe** a piece of seaweed. **ware sea** a heavy sea which casts seaweed ashore. **ware pick** a bent pick for gathering seaweed.

wark *n.* **1** work. **2** on goings, especially *wild wark* violent on

goings. **3** a fuss. *'A lot o wark aboot nothing.'* **4** other things in addition, *'Whit wi this football and wark, he's hardly ever home.'*

warran *v.* warrant. *'I'se warran.'* *'I warran thee for hid'* I'm certain that's true. *'He'll no be aback o askan, I'se warran'* I'm certain that he will not be too shy to ask. (*warran* was used frequently at one time).

wartie girse *n.* sun spurge. (the milky fluid from the hollow stem supposedly cures warts).

wash *v.p.t.* **wush, washed** wash. *'I wush aal day yesterday and got aal me washeen dry.'*

washie *n.* a small cod.

wast *n.* west.

watch *v.* **1** watch. **2** notice, see. *'I watched his daeth in the paper.'*

watter *n.* water. *tae wade the watter* or *tae be through the watter* referring to passage through life's troubles, *'Wir been through the watter and we ken hoo deep hid is.'* **watter-arro, watter-arvo** common chickweed. **watter-berge** see BERGE. **watter-blot** rinsing water. **watter-hen** a moor hen. (in Ork *moor hen* is reserved for the red grouse). **watter-pleep** the snipe. **watter-traa** heartburn. **wattery-pleeps** the redshank. **wattery-wagtail** the pied wagtail, so called because it is supposedly a sign of rainy weather if it comes near the house. **wattereens** *n.* a watering hole for cattle in the old days.

wather see **weather.**

wazzie *n.* **1** a band of twisted straw used as a collar for a horse or ox. **2** a round flat straw cushion formerly used by stone breakers etc. **3** a cylindrical stool. **4** a bundle of tightly twisted wool etc. **5** a scarf.

weareen claes *n.* working clothes.

weather, wather *n.* weather. **weather blinks** distant flashes of lightning in the sky too far away for thunder to be heard. (also known as **spunkies** or **wild fire**). **weather-kind** a cloudy sky betokening a rainstorm but which is unlikely to materialise. **wather-moose** a twitch in the eye. (also known as a **life corn**). **wather gauge, weather gauge** a barometer, *tae get the wather gauge o somebody* to get the upper hand. **weather-mooth** a point on the horizon from which clouds apparently radiate indicating the *mouth* from which the weather is coming. The clouds are in fact parallel and appear to radiate because of perspective.

weedow *n.* widow. **weedow-wife** widow. **weedow-man** widower.

weefle *v.* shake. **weeflie** *adj.* shaky, wavering.

weegaldie-waggaldie *adj.* unsteady.

week *n.* the corner of the mouth, generally in the plural. *'Clean thee weeks bairn.'* **tae be doon i the weeks** to look sad.

weel *adj.* well. **weel said** truly said. *'Hid's weel said he's no tae be trusted.'*

weeman *n.* women, used as a plural of wife (*wan wife, two weeman*).

weengle *v.* swing around, particularly of a child balancing his chair on two legs, *'Stop weenglan on that chair beuy!'* **tae weengle something oot o somebody** to wheedle it out.

weenklie *adj.* unstable, bending. **weenkle-wankle** *'He wis walkan weenkle-wankle.'*

weeo *n.* a kittiwake.

weesk, wheesk *v.* **1** (of a door or a mouse) squeak. **2** whisper. **3** (of a dog) make a high pitched whine. *n.* a squeak.

weesko[1] *n.* an oilcan.

weesko[2], **weeskal, weeso, weeslo, wheeso, wisoo** *n.* a tangled mass of threads.

weester *v.* squeak.

weet *adj.* wet. **tae maak weet** to rain.

weh *v.* make a moaning noise as if in pain. *'A ferfil wehan soond kam fae ahint the press.'* **weh** *n.* a moaning noise.

welt *n.* speed *tae go at full welt.*

wentid *adj.* flat tasting (e.g. lemonade, home brew).

wersy *adj.* **1** feeling off colour. **2** thin, weak, *gey wersy soup.*

wey[1] *n.* way.

wey[2] *v.* weigh. **tae wey salt** an old game in which two competitors would stand back to back and with the arms linked lift each other alternatively off the ground until one of the pair gives in.

whaap *n.* a curlew.

whacker *n.* outstanding in size etc., '*Beuy that's a right whacker o a baest.*' **whackan** *adj.* big.

whacko see **quackoo.**

whaese *v.* pant.

whamsy *adj.* queasy, seasick.

whar[1] *pron.* who. '*Whar's that gaan along the road?*' Who is that going along the road?

whar[2] *conj.* where. **wharpiece** where? '*Wharpiece are yi gaan?.*'

wharr *v.* make a rattling noise in the throat.

whark *v.* cough up, *tae whark and spit.*

whassigo *n.* **1** insincere talk. **2** an excuse. **3** a fancy or craze. **4** a person who creates a fuss over unimportant things.

wheek *v.* snatch, '*Beuy afore I could deu anything he wheekid hid oot o me hand.*'

wheel-gut *n.* the long small bowel of a sheep formerly used as a driving band on a spinning wheel. **wheel-spow** only in *tae go wheel-spow* to turn a cartwheel.

wheenk *v.* toss the head or jerk the body expressively, especially *tae wheenk and laugh. n.* a flounce.

wheer, whaar *v.* wheeze, '*The cowld's gin doon on his breest noo and he's just wheeran.*'

wheest, wheesht *exclam.* 'Be quiet!'; also '*Had yir wheest!*'

wheisa-girse *n.* ground-elder.

wheou *n.* the sound made by the wind whistling through the chinks of a closed door.

whesso *n.* goutweed. The roots and leaves were boiled and used as a poultice in case of gout.

whewan, wheean *adj.* (of the wind) howling round corners.

whid *n.* a peculiarity of temper.

whiddie *adj.* **1** (of a wind) changing direction. **2** (of people or animals) temperamental.

whill *conj.* until, '*Bide there whill I come.*'

whin[1] *n.* gorse.

whin[2] *n.* hard stone, especially, *blue whin* hard flag stone with a bluish colour.

whirlygigger *n.* whirlygig.

whiss, whizz *v.* quiz, ask questions in a forthright (and inquisitive) manner.

whit *pron.* what **whit wey** how. '*Whitwey deu I get oot o here noo?*' **Whit wey hid?**, Why not? e.g. '*Ah'm no gaan tae the toon the morn efter aal.*' '*Whit wey hid?.*' **whit a** a curtailed form of *whit a lot o* e.g. '*Whit a kye in the mart the day,*' What a lot of cattle in the mart today. '*Whit o'clock is hid?*' What time is it? **whit time?** when? '*Whit time are yi gan oot?*' **whitan** what, '*Whitan bonny flooers!*' **whit-like** how?, especially in the common social greeting '*Whit like the day?*' How are you today? **whitna** what? as in, '*Whitna man is that?*' **whitnafura** what kind of? '*Whitnafura jam is this on the table?.*'

white *v.p.t.* **whet** quit. '*White hid noo!*' Stop it at once! '*Ah'm whet gaan tae the sea noo. Ah'm too owld beuy!*'

whitemaa *n.* a seagull.

whitna see **whit**.

whull, whullo, whill see **quill**.

whummle *v.* overturn.

whup *v.* **1** whip. **2** snatch. '*He whuppid the knife oot o me hand.*' *n.* a snatch.

wid¹ *v.* would (see also **wad**). **widna, widno** would not. '*I widna say*' I tend to agree with you.

wid², wud *n.* wood.

wife *n.* **1** wife. **2** woman. (the plural of *wife* is *weeman*; 'woman' is used only vocatively and familiarly in Ork dial when it is pronounced *wumman* or *umman* '*Come on umman!*' Come on dear!). **owld wife 1** used of a man who gossips and shows excessive interest in other people's affairs, '*He's just a owld wife.*' **2** a hag or witch; **tae free the owld wife** an expression used at sea when fishing cuithes. After three cuithes had been landed the fisherman had *freed the owld wife*.

wifflo *n.* snag.

wight *n.* **1** weight. **2** blame. '*Thoo'll hiv tae tak the wight for hid.*'

wild duck *n.* a mallard. **wild fire** lightning without thunder.

wilk *n.* **1** whelk. **2** the nickname of an inhabitant of Wyre.

Wilkie *n.* a spirit which inhabited certain mounds in Westray and which was periodically given an offering of milk poured through a hole in the top of the mound.

will *v.* lose one's way, also **tae go will. willan** wandering in the mind. **willsome** *adj.* speaking of e.g. a hill, '*That's a willsome hill*' i.e. a hill with no paths where it is easy to get lost in the dark.

Willie-long-legs *n.* daddy long legs or the crane fly. **Willie-wabster** a spider. **tae work Willie Hay's wark** to be up to mischief (Westray). **Willie Heron** the heron.

win *v.p.t.* **wan** *p.p.* **wun 1** win. **2** make one's way, reach. '*I couldna win tae the toon fur me car broke doon.*' '*The door wis locked and I couldna win in.*' **3** defeat. '*We'll win yi.*'

wind *n.* **1** the wind, '*Ah'm heard the wind blowan afore*' I don't believe you will do what you say you will. **2** air, '*I must pit some wind in me tyres.*' **wind bird, wind cuffer** the kestrel. (from its habit of hovering in the air when searching for prey). **wind-blether** a sea-shell. **wind-feeder** a shower which brings with it an increase in the wind's strength. **windrift** ruin or destruction '*Hid's aa gin tae windrift.*' **wind-skew** a board with a long stick attached to it, used to change the draught in the open central flue of the Old Orkney house. **windthrush** the redwing. **windy** a call by schoolboys when a player of the opposite team kicks a ball out of play, sarcastically suggesting that the breach has been caused by the wind. **windy-whistle** an acute pain in the front teeth occurring naturally or caused by inhaling air rapidly through them.

winder *v.* wonder. '*I winder tae me if he's any happier.*' '*I widna winder bit he's gin home.*' I think he's gone home.

windleen, winleen *n.* an bundle of hay or straw tied with its own ends.

window-sole *n.* window-sill.

winkie *n.* the little finger.

wint, wunt *adj.* accustomed, wont. '*He's wint wae that*', '*He's ower-weel wint*' He's too accustomed to having the best, said of a child over fussy about his food etc. *n.* custom, habit. **tae pit somebody in a bad wint** to introduce someone to something he/she should not experience. '*Don't gae the bairn wine, hid'll pit her in a bad wint.*'

winya, winyo *n.* destruction or ruin, '*Hid's all gin tae winyo.*'

wir¹, wur *pron.* our. '*This is wir youngest son.*' **wirs, wurs** *pron.* ours. **wirsaels, wursaels** ourselves. **wiroos, wuroos** our house.

wir², wur *pron.+v.* we are. '*Wir coman ower the morn.*'

wir³, wur *v.p.t.* were, was '*I wir sure hid wis thee.*'

wire-grass *n.* couch grass.

wirk, work *v. p.t.* **wrowt 1** work. **2** be employed (at), '*He wrowt at Gorn a whiley.*' **3** (of ale) ferment. **tae wirk a sock** to knit a sock. **tae work the creels** to fish lobsters. **tae wirk a wark 1** to be busy about something, '*Whit a wark he's wirkan doon there at the corner*' (he was building a house). **2** to make mischief, '*Whit a wark that young fulloos were wirkan at Edwin's last night*', (they were playing Hallowe'en pranks). **3** to behave in an odd way, '*Every time I stert me car hid splutters an wirks a wark.*' **wirkeen** working; *tae go fae wirkeen* of machinery etc to break down.

wi, wae *prep.* **1** with. **2** by. *tae go wi the bus, car etc* to go by bus, car etc. **wi** (used vocatively) '*Gae me a box o matches wi thee.*'

withershins *adv.* in an anticlockwise direction, '*Hid's bad luck beuy tae turn the boat withershins.*'

witty *adj.* witty, sane. **no witty** crazy.

wiz *n.* ways, only in '*Come thee wiz*', 'Come this way,' used particularly as a warm invitation to a visitor in the sense 'Come in.'

woggie-kattie-mattie *n.* noughts and crosses. (origin unknown but must be an ancient form; see **trip-trap-truiskie**).

word, wird *n.* word. **tae hiv words** to have an argument. **tae come intae words** to get round to talking about something. '*I don't ken whit wey hid kam intae wirds*' I don't know how we came to speak of it.

worm (the) *n.* toothache. (from the belief that it was caused by a worm).

wumman, umman *n.* woman, a familiar form of address to a lady. '*Come on wumman.*'

wummle *n.* a gimlet. A rhyme used in tickling a child is:-
Haet a wummle, bore a hole,
Whar piece, whar piece?
Just there, there, there!

wun¹ *n.* a pleasure, '*Hid's a wun tae see thee, lass.*'

wun² see **win.**

wup *n.* **1** a turn round, coil. '*Tak a wup roond the bollard wi the rope.*' **2** a journey up and down with a plough. '*Mercy I hid done only two wup when the rain kam on.*' **wup, wip** *v.* wind round, bind.

wur see **wir.**

Y

ya, yaa *exclam.* Yes, '*Are yi gaan the morn?*' '*Ya.*' **yaase 1** yes. **2** Hello! especially in the phrase commonly used among males, '*Yaase min!*' **yass** North Isles form of *yaase.*

yackle *n.* molar tooth. '*He's cut all his yackles*' he wasn't born yesterday. *v.* chew.

yaggle *v.* **1** chew laboriously at something or to work laboriously at something. **2** make a mess of cutting something (eg cloth). '*Thoo're makin a naafil yaggle wi that blunt shears.*'

yam *n.* **1** the large mussel (*modiolus vulgaris*) dredged up for bait. **2** an old type of potato grown in Orkney not unlike Kerr's Pink.

yammals, yammalds, yamils *n.* people of the same age, '*Me and Bob are yammals, we wir in the sam class at the school.*'

yap *v.* **1** bark. **2** talk incessantly. *n.* someone who talks insistently. **yap o dirt** a persistent talker.

yarfa, yarfie paet *n.* peat cut with a heather crown, only one peat deep. Two cartloads of *yarfa peat* were burned and the ash used to manure the **plantie creu** annually.

yarg *v.* nag.

yarm *v.* **1** (of a cat) mew plaintively. **2** (of a sheep) bleat (North Ronaldsay). **3** complain in a whining way.

yatter *v.* chatter.

year *n.* year (pronounced *ear*). The plural of ear (year) is *ear* if it immediately follows a numeral e.g. *a hunder ear* but, *hunders o ears.*

yeask *n.* a squeaking sound made with difficulty. '*I wis so krome I could hardly mak a yeask.*'

yellow, yalla, yilloo *adj.* yellow. **yellow fish** smoked fish. **yellow gowan** marsh marigold. **yellow lily** yellow iris. **yellow yarleen** the bird, yellow hammer.

yerneens, yirneens, yirnam *n.* **1** rennet. **2** a nickname for the people of Orphir. It is said the name stems from an Orphir lady who made rennet commercially. **yirn** *v.* form curds to make cheese.

yetleen *n.* an iron girdle used for baking, once hung on a *cruik* but now used on the top of cookers.

yig, yug *v.* tug, pull sharply. *n.* a tug, sharp pull.

yin *pron.* that (common in the North Isles of Orkney) '*My whar's yin?*'

yir¹ *pron.* your.

yir² *pron.+v.* you are.

yirg, yerg *v. & n.* jerk, tug.

yivverie *adj.* keen on, eager *'Ah'm no very yivverie for this ebb-maet.'*

yoke *v.* grasp firmly.

yolder, yalder *v.* make a loud noise like a dog being hurt. **yolderan and singan** with emphasis on volume rather than tune, applied for example to a drunk person.

yole *n.* a small undecked fishing boat with two masts and a jib.

yowe *n.* ewe.

yug, yog *n.* the large mussel.

yuik, yuck *v.* itch. **yuikie** *adj.* itchy. **yuikie stone** a protruding stone at shoulder level in an old Orkney house and used for itching the back.

Yule *n.* Christmas time.

Yule-girs *n.* the plant meadow-sweet.

Yule-skrep *n.* a smack on the bottom.

A

abandon *v.* tyne.
abort *v.* (of animals) cast.
about *prep.* aboot.
above *prep.* abuin, abune.
abuse *v.* lay oot for, misca, spaek ill o.
accident *n.* misanter.
accompany *v.* follow.
according *adv.* accorned.
account *n.* accoont.
accustomed *adj.* wint.
ache *v.* tift.
acquainted *adj.* acquent.
active *adj.* sturtsome.
add (to) *v.* eek. **addition** *n.* eek.
additionally *adv,* forbye.
adze *n.* fiteetch.
afraid *adj.* faerd.
after *prep.* efter.
afternoon *n,* efternuin.
against *prep.* fornent.
age *n.* (same) aboot ages, yammals.
agile *adj.* swack.
agitated *adj.* up tae high doh.
ahead *adv.* aheid.
ailing *adj.* trowie.
aimless person *n.* knotless threid.
alive *adj.* livan, tae the fore.
all *adj.* aa, aal.
almost *adv.* nearaboot.
also *adv.* teu, forbye.
always *adv.* aye, alwis.
amble *v.* dolder, dander, andoo, drilt.
an *ind. art.* a.
anger *v.* get een's birse ap. *n.* madrom.
angry *adj.* mad, barman.
ankles *n.* cuits.
annoyed *adj.* at-pitten, grabbid.

another *adj.* anither.
ant *n.* myro.
anti-clockwise *adv.* withershins.
anyhow *adv.* anywey.
anywhere *adv.* anywey, anypiece.
apart *adv.* sindrie.
apart from *prep.* unless, forbye.
appearance *n.* atfers.
apple *n.* epple.
approach *n.* (method) atgyong.
April Fool! *exclam.* Gock, gock! Hintie gock! **April Fool's Day** Gockeen Day.
apron *n.* peenie, bratto.
arctic skua *n.* skootie-allan.
arctic tern *n.* pickie-terno.
argue *v.* thraep at. **arguing** caunglan.
argumentative *adj.* ill-vetrit.
arm *n.* erm. **armpit** *n.* oxter.
around *prep.* aroond.
arse *n.* erse.
artful *adj.* fly.
ash *n.* ass, ess.
ashamed *adj.* affrontid.
ask *v.* speer.
askew *adv.* skaoowaoo, skeewif, glyed.
asleep *adj.* sleepan.
astern *adv.* astarn.
astride *adv.* stridielegs.
asunder *adv.* sindrie.
at all *adv.* ava.
attack *v.* light on.
August *n.* Aagist.
aurora borealis *n.* Merry Dancers.
awake *adj.* wakkened.
away *adv.* awey, awa.
awful *adj.* aafil, bonny, godless.

awkward *adj.* aakward, ill-thraan, thraan, tirrie, twirnie.
awn *n.* aan, skegg.

axe *n.* exe, eetch.
axle *n.* exle.

B

babble *v.* haiver.
back *n.* (of a person) keel, riggeen.
back to front *adv.* backside foremost, erse aboot face.
background *n.* backgrund.
backward *adj.* a-back.
backwards *adv.* backleens, erseleens.
backwash *n.* backsook.
badly behaved *adj.* ill-answeran.
bad-tempered *adj.* tirrie, twartie, twirnie-faced.
bag *n.* pock.
bale *v.* owse.
ball *n.* ba, baal. (of wool) clew.
bang *n.* ding, dunk.
barnacle *n.* kleck, sea-geese, slykees.
barnacle-goose *n.* kleck-goose.
barrow *n.* borrow, burroo.
bashful *adj.* blate.
basket *n.* cubbie.
basking shark *n.* hoe-mither.
bathe *n.* dook.
beach *n.* shore. *v.* haal.
beak *n.* neb.
beat *v.* baet.
because *conj.* caes.
become *v.* get.
beetle *n.* gablo.
before *prep.* afore.
beg *v.* peese.
began *v.p.t.* begood.
behaviour *n.* atfers.
behind *prep.* ahint.

belch *v. & n.* rift.
bellow *v.* bogle, gowl. *n.* bogle.
belly *n.* puggie.
beneath *prep.* anunder.
bent *adj.* (of a person) crappened ap.
berate *v.* flyte on.
better looking *adj.* better like.
beside *prep.* aside.
besides *adv.* forbye.
between *prep.* atween.
big *adj.* muckle.
bind *v.* wup.
binoculars *n.* spyglesses.
bird's foot trefoil *n.* cocks and hens.
bitch *n.* bikko.
black-backed gull *n.* baakie, swarbie, swartback.
blackbird *n.* blackie.
black guillemot *n.* tyst, sinnie fynnie.
black-headed gull *n.* heidie craa, ritto, swarfarro, black hatto.
blast *n.* (of wind) gowster.
blaze *v.* aize, lowe. *n.* lowe.
bleat *v.* maa.
bleed *v.* bluid.
blenny *n.* swarfish, swirdie.
bless *v.* bliss. **blessings** *n.* blisseens.
blind *v.* (with light) blinder.
blister *n.* blibe, bleb.
blizzard *n.* moor, smook.
blow *n.* clipe, dad, dunt, pelt, lander. *v.* bla. (of snow) fann, smook, smoor.

bluebottle *n.* fishie-flee, matlo.
boat *n.* bott, (small) pram, quill, flattie, yole.
boat-shelter *n.* noust.
bobbin *n.* purm.
bog cotton *n.* Lucky Minnie's oo.
boil *v.* ramp.
boisterous *adj.* rugfus.
bolt *v.* (door etc.) snib.
boot *n.* buit. **boot-polish** buit-blekk.
boredom *n.* langer.
borrow *v.* git a len o.
botch up *n.* clatch ap.
bother *n.* trachle. *v.* humbug.
bottom *n.* buddum, boddom.
bought *v.p.t.* bowt.
bounce *v.* stott.
boundary *n.* mairch.
bow (of a boat) *n.* boo, nose.
bowels *n.* booels.
bradawl *n.* borag.
brand-new *adj.* spleet-new.
brass *n.* bress.
brat *n.* nickum.
bread *n.* lof.
break *v.* brak. **breakable** *adj.* frush.
breast *n.* breist.

brent (goose) *n.* quink.
bridge *n.* brig.
bridle *n.* branks.
bring *v.* tak.
broke *v.p.t.* bruik.
broken *adj.* brakken, puggled.
brood *v.* (of hens) cluck. **broody hen** cluckan hen.
brother *n.* brither.
brown *adj.* broon. (of wool) moorit.
bruise *v.* murder.
brush *n.* besom.
brushwood *n.* rice, rysos.
budge *v.* imse.
build *v.* big. **building** *n.* biggeen.
bulge *v.* shuit, shut.
bullock *n.* stott.
bump *v.* dird.
bun *n.* cookie.
burn *v.* lowe. **burnt** *p.p.* brunt.
burst *v.p.t.* spret.
bush *n.* buss.
busy *adj.* thrang.
butt *v.* doose.
butterwort *n.* eccle girse, klepsie girse.
butterfly *n.* kailieflee.

C

cabbage *n.* kail, keel. **cabbage plot** *n.* kailie-creu.
cackle *v.* claek, clank.
call *v.* caa.
cap *n.* kep, coolie.
capability *n.* gis.
capsize *v.* coop.
caraway *n.* carvey.
careless *adj.* ram-stam, gushlan.
carry *v.* caerry, humph.

carry-on *n.* on-gaans, wark.
case *n.* caes.
catapult *n.* plushnie.
caterpillar *n.* heatherie-brottick, kailie-worm.
cattle *n.* kye, kye-baest, baest, animals.
caught *v.p.t.* catched.
centipede *n.* Jennie-hunder-legs, forty-feeter.

chair *n.* stuil. **Orkney chair** *n.* strae-backid stuil.

challenge *v.* brett ap tae.

chamber pot *n.* chantie.

change *v.* (of wind) cast aboot. *n.* (of wind) aboot-cast. **changeable** *adj.* (of wind) whiddie.

chapped *adj.* pickid, hackid.

charlock *n.* runcho, bresso.

chase *v.* chaest.

chatter *v.* blether, lay aff, yap, yatter.

chatter-box *n.* blether, bletherskate, trattle-bogie.

cheat *v.* chaet, swick.

cheerful *adj.* lightsome.

chest *n.* girnal, kist.

chew *v.* chow, nyavse, yackle, yaggle.

chickenpox *n.* nirls.

chickweed *n.* arvo, ervo, water-arro.

chilblains *n.* fissies.

child *n.* bairn, nacket. **children** *n.* bairns, cheelders.

childish *adj.* bairnlie.

chimney *n.* chimley, lum.

china *n.* laem, leem.

chives *n.* syes, syves.

choke *v.* thrapple, go doon the wrong hass.

choppy sea *n.* jabble.

churn *v. & n.* kirn.

clamber *v.* climmer.

claws *n.* cluiks.

clean out *v.* dight, ripe oot.

clear out *v.* redd ap.

climb *v.* clim, climmer.

clod *n.* divot.

close *adv.* closs. **close by** aboot hands wi. **closely related** sib.

cloth *n.* cloot. **clothes** *n.* claes.

clover *n.* smero, kippacks. **red**

clover curlie doddie.

clumsy *adj.* cuffy, feeflie, footeran, handless, skefflie. **clumsy person** *n.* gushel, footer. **clumsy thing** *n.* klumbung.

coalfish *n.* sillock, cuithe, piltick, cuitheen, doondie.

coarse *adj.* coorse.

coated *adj.* barkit, laggered.

coax *v.* tise.

cobweb *n.* moose-wab.

coil *v.* hank, wup. *n.* wup.

cold *adj.* cowld, cauld. **cold breeze** *n.* cuil.

colourful *adj.* rorie, skyran.

coltsfoot *n.* tishalago.

comb *v.* redd. *n.* redder.

comedown *n.* dooncome.

common-sense *n.* gis, gy, mither-wit.

commotion *n.* wap.

compensation *n.* upmak.

competence *n.* gis, gy.

competent *adj.* reddly.

complain *v.* girn, pleep.

completely *adv.* clean, ferly.

conceited *adj.* bigsie, prinky.

condition *n.* had.

confusion *n.* steer, steero.

considerable *adj.* (size, distance etc.) dainty.

contagious *adj.* smitsome.

cool *adj. & v.* cuil.

coot *n.* sneeshan, snellie, synsin.

cormorant *n.* hibleen, lerblade, skarf.

corn-bunting *n.* skitter-broltie, thistlecock.

couch-grass *n.* sinnie-girse.

cough *v.* host. **cough up phlegm** *v.* aak, hack, whark.

count *v.* coont. **counter** *n.* coonter.

counting-out rhyme *n.* saetro.
cousin *n.* coseen.
cow *n.* coo, (pl. kye). **cowpat** *n.* coo's plirt, skon. **cow dung** sharn.
coward *n.* faerdie.
cow parsley *n.* chocksie, kecko, spurrie-girse.
cowrie-shell *n.* grottie-buckie.
cowshed *n.* byre.
crab *n.* ersie-crab, fimlar crab, kleppispur, partan.
cram *v.* stap.
crank *n.* (handle) wap.
crash *n.* skelder, skelliment.
crawling with *adj.* hudjan.
crazy *adj.* gyte, no witty, uim.
crease *n.* lirk.
creature *n.* craetir.
cripple *n.* limiter.
crook *n.* cruik.
cross *adj.* mad, tirrie, twartie.
cross-beam *n.* (roof)back, twartback. (boat) thaft.

cross-wise *adv.* twartleens.
crouch *v.* go doon on the hookers, cruggle.
crow *v. & n.* craa.
crowberry *n.* heather berry.
crowd *n.* dreef, skorie, skry.
crumble *v.* mulder. **crumbs** *n.* mulders.
crumbly *adj.* brucklie, frush.
crunch *v.* krow.
cry *v.* greet, tak tae the eyes. **cried** *p.t.* gret. **crying** *adj.* greetan, tizzan.
cry baby *n.* freck, poort.
cuckoo *n.* gock.
cultivate *v.* brak oot.
cupboard *n.* aumrie, press.
curdle *v.* (cheese) yirn. **curdled** *adj.* (good) yirned. (bad) lappered.
curlew *n.* whaap.
curt *adj.* nippit.
curtain *n.* coorteen.
cut *v.* (peats etc.) share.
cuttlefish *n.* skeeto.

D

daisy *n.* cockalowrie.
dam *v.* tepp *n.* teppin.
damage *v.* misacker.
dandelion *n.* dog flooer.
dangle *v.* dilder.
darkness *n.* mirk.
daughter *n.* dowter.
dawdle *v.* drilt.
daze *n.* dwam.
dead *adj.* deid.
deaf *adj.* daef. **deafen** *v.* daive.
decay *v.* moze. **decayed** *adj.* mozie.
decent *adj.* daesent.

decorations *n.* eerie-orums, veerie-orums.
deduce *v.* jalouse.
delay *n.* aff-pit, pit-aff.
dent *v. & n.* dint.
derelict *adj.* unfaandoon, geen tae skatfa.
deserved *adj.* amis.
destruction *n.* geldro.
devil *n.* deil.
diarrhoea *n.* back-door trot, scoor, skitter.
did *v.p.t.* did, duid.
die *v.* dee.

difference *n.* differ.
difficulty *n.* trachle. **difficult** *adj.* no aesy.
dig *v.* dell. (out) hock.
dilapidated *adj.* homeward-bound.
dip *v.* dimmle. *n.* dook.
direction *n.* aert.
dirty *adj.* eltit, suckie, barkit. *v.* elt.
disagreeable *adj.* twartie.
disagreeing *adj.* caunglan.
disappointed *adj.* grypid.
disappointment *n.* sook-in.
disgust *v.* scunner.
dishevelled *adj.* ravsie, tagsie.
disintegrating *adj.* unfaansindrie.
distance *n.* piece.
ditch *n.* grip, (small) trink.
diver *n.* (great northern) emmergoose. (red-throated) loon, raingoose.
dizzy *adj.* heidlight.
do *v.* do, dae, deu.
dock (bot.) *n.* dochan, bulwand, tirso.
dogfight *n.* hassfang.
dogfish *n.* hoe, daa, blind daa.
dog-whelk *n.* cattie-buckie.
done *v.p.p.* done, din.
doubt *n.* doot. **doubtful** *adj.* dootfil, jubish.

dovecote *n.* doocot.
down *adv.* doon.
downpour *n.* doonpoor, demption, ootfa.
dozen *num.* dizzen.
drag *v.* draig.
draw *v.* draa. **drawer** *n.* draaer.
drain *v.* sye. *n.* syer.
drainage *n.* (channel) oddler, sester, runnick. (boat) nile.
dreadful *adj.* aafil, humlan.
drenched *adj.* drockit, drookled, sabbid. **drenching** *n.* drockeen.
dried up *adj.* gizzened, rivven.
drift *v.* (snow) fann, moor.
drill *n.* dreel.
drive *v.* (sheep etc.) caa.
drizzle *n.* dister, driv, rug. **drizzling** *adj.* ruggie
drop *v. & n.* drap.
drought *n.* drooth, drowth, sook.
drunk *adj.* blootered, styman. drucken. **drunken** *adj.* drucken.
dry *v.* toin. (fish) sook.
ducking *n.* dook.
dung *n.* sharn.
dunlin *n.* plover page, boondie.
dusk *n.* grimleens.
dust *n.* coom, stoor.
dwell *v.* bide.

E

eager *adj.* yivverie.
ear *n.* lug. (of corn) aicher.
early *adv.* bi time.
earth *n.* muild.
earthenware *n.* laem, leem.
earwig *n.* forkie-tail, spurrie, teddrie-tail, muiro.

ease *v.* aese. **easy** *adj.* aesy.
east *n.* aest.
eat *v.* aet. (hungrily) gafse. (noisily) chapse.
eaves *n.* aisins.
economise *v.* hain.
effect *n.* feck.

eider *n.* dunter.
eight *num.* ight (as in English *right*).
  eighteen ighteen. **eighty** ighty.
either *prep.* ither.
elaborate *adj.* fantoosh.
elder tree *n.* boorwid, boortree.
ember *n.* ammer.
empty *adj.* tuim. *v.* tuim.
empty handed *adj.* bare-handed.
end *n.* hinderend.
endure *v.* thole.
energy *n.* thrift.
enough *adv.* enoff, anyoch.
enquire *v.* speer.
entice *v.* tise.
entirely *adv.* clean, ferly.
equal *adj.* upsides wi.
especially *adv.* ferfil.

everybody *pron.* aabody.
ewe *n.* yowe. (young) gimmer. (old)
  cast yowe.
excellent *adj.* parteeclar.
except *prep.* unless.
exchange *v.* coze.
excited *adj.* heysk, up tae high doh.
excitement *n.* heyse, stram.
excrement *n.* cack, keech.
exhaust *v.* (oneself) breekse.
exhausted *adj.* deeskit, breeksed,
  oot-mochted, puggled.
expect *v.* lippen.
extinguish *v.* slock.
extremely *adv.* humlan.
eye *n.* eye, ee. **eyes** een. (in shoes
  etc.) pie-holes.
eye-bright (bot.) *n.* bright-eye.

F

fair *n.* market.
fairy *n.* hill-trow, sea-trow, hogboy.
fairies *n.* Finfolk. **Fairy-land** *n.*
  Hildaland.
Faith! *exclam.* fegs, feth, heth.
fall *v. & n.* faa.
fancy *n.* gee, notion. *adj.* fantoosh.
farm *n.* ferm. **farmer** *n.* fermer.
farm buildings *n.* steedeen.
farther *adv.* farder.
fastening *n.* tyal. (door) sneck,
  tirler.
father *n.* faether.
fatherlasher *n.* uiko.
fault *n.* faalt. **faulty** *adj.* faalty.
feeble *adj.* peelie-wallie.
feed *v.* (animals) maet, supper.
fencing post *n.* stab.
fester *v.* beel, bael.
fever *n.* fivver.

few *num.* twa, twartree.
field *n.* park, tumal, sheed.
filthy *adj.* eltit, clartid, filtie.
fine *adj.* braa.
finish *v. & n.* feeneesh.
fire *n.* (roaring) aizer, eezer. **set fire
  to** set lowe tae.
fishing-line *n.* darrow, snuid.
  fishing-rod wand.
fist *n.* naive.
fit *adj.* swack.
flame *n.* lowe.
flash *n.* bluisk.
flew *v.p.t.* fled.
flimsy *adj.* trindlie.
floor-board *n.* (boat) tulfer.
flounce *n.* fleenk.
flounder *n.* (fish) fluik.
flour *n.* flooer.
flower *n.* flooer.

fluency/fluent speech *n.* aff-lay.
fly *v.* flee. *n.* flee, fleeo.
fold *n.* fald, lirk.
folk *n.* fock.
food *n.* maet.
fool *n.* fuil, gappus, guip, nout, taupie-goat. *v.* (make a fool of) guip, gock, tak the wag o.
foolish *adj.* fuilie, gleckit, kringlie-heided.
foot *n.* feet. **footwear** feetwear.
foraging *adj.* fendan.
ford *n.* waddie.
found *v.p.t.* fund, fand.
foundation *n.* found, steethe.
founder *v.* funder.
four *num.* fower.
foxglove *n.* trowie-girse.

fragments *n.* mummie, scows, shellmaleens, skroo, smook, smush.
freckle *n.* fairnteckle.
fresh *adj.* (of milk) sweet.
fretful *adj.* girnie, pleepie.
friable *adj.* brucklie, frush.
friend *n.* freend.
fright *n.* fleg, gluff, flix.
frighten *v.* fleg, flix. **frightened** *adj.* faerd, skarr.
from *prep.* fae.
full *adj.* fill, lippan.
fulmar *n.* mallimak.
funnel *n.* filler.
furrow *n.* furr.
fuss *v.* (make a fuss) freck. *n.* caa tae, wark.
fussy *adj.* tefferie.

G

gable *n.* breist, gavel, gavel-end.
gad about *v.* stravaig, vaig, dander.
gale *n.* skuther o wind, skirler, skreever.
games dicky-doo, faily fight, gildro, flay the cat, gaadie, geepie-gawpie, huppidy-drolty/craa, pedro, trip-trap-truisky, wey (weigh) saalt, sweerie stick, pogo, pen-gun, woggie-kattie-mattie, picko, square-tree, tig, tirlo, skirlo, snorry-bone.
gander *n.* ganner.
garden *n.* gaerdeen.
gargle *v.* hurkle.
garrulous person *n.* bletherskate.
garters *n.* gerteens.
gasp *v.* whaese.
gate *n.* gett, slap.

gather *v.* gaether, hint.
gaunt *adj.* hockit.
gave *v.p.t.* gaed, geed, gid.
gaze *v.* gan.
get *v.* git. **get down to** set face tae. **get to somewhere** win tae. **get away from** win fae.
ghost *n.* ganfer, bawkie.
giant *n.* Tammy o Tirlybraes, Hug Boy, Cubbie Roo, Thing wi the wan Eye, Lucky Minni, Grullyan
giddy *adj.* heidlight.
gift *n.* faireen, mindeen.
giggle *v.* gilder, galder, cheeter.
gimlet *n.* wummle.
girl *n.* lass.
give *v.* gae. **given** *p.p.* gaen, geen, gin.
gizzard *n.* goosrin.

glad *adj.* gled, blide.
glance *n.* teet, keek.
glass *n.* gless. **glasses** glesses.
glimpse *n.* glisk.
gloaming *n.* grimleens.
glove *n.* gliv.
go *v.* go, gae, gyung. **going** *pres.p.* gaan. **gone** *p.p.* gaen, geen, gin.
golden eye duck *n.* gowdie duck.
golden plover *n.* pliver.
good-for-nothing *adj.* deuless.
Goodness knows! *exclam.* Best kens.
Goodness me! *exclam.* Good! Good bliss me! Mercy me! Mighty me! Lokkars! Beuy! Loshans!
goosander *n.* saw-bill.
goose-grass *n.* sticky-willie.
gorse *n.* whin.
gossip *v.* claek, gab, clash. *n.* bletherskate.
gossiping *adj.* newsan.
grab *v.* gramse, veeze a had o.
grass *n.* gress, girse, fussie-punds.
grassland *n.* ley.

great northern diver *n.* emmer goose.
greedy *adj.* gloondie, skatfo.
griddle *n.* yetleen.
grind *v.* (teeth) share.
grope *v.* glomer.
ground *n.* grund. *v.* (of boat) grund, buddum.
ground-elder *n.* wheisa-girse.
grouse *n.* mirren, moor-hen.
growling *adj.* nauran.
grumble *v.* girn, pleep.
grunt *v.* grink.
guarantee *v.* warran.
guess *v.* giss, jalouse.
guillemot *n.* (common) aak, skoot, (black) tyst, tystie.
gull *n.* maa, whitemaa, skorie.
gullet *n.* hass.
gulp *v.* glunt, glup, gulup, glaip.
gurgle *v.* chilter, sweenkle.
gurnard *n.* krooner, horsegornick.
gust *v.* batt, flan, swap. *n.* dud, gowster, swap.
gusty *adj.* thuddie.
guttering *n.* rone, spoot.

H

habit *n.* wint.
had *v.p.t.* haed, heed.
hailstone *n.* hailie-puckle.
halter *n.* branks.
halves *n.* halfers.
halfway *adv.* halfleens, half road.
hand *v.* shaa.
handful *n.* guipen.
hang *v.* hing.
happy *adj.* blide.
harvest *n.* hervest, hairst. **harvest time** *n.* back-end.

haul *v.* haal.
have *v.* hae, hiv.
hay *n.* hey. **haycock** cole.
hazy *adj.* imy.
head *n.* heid. **headlong** *adv.* heidleens, afore a face. **head to tail** heids an traas.
headstrong *adj.* ram-stam.
heap *n.* haep, bing, brook, roo, clash, rookle. *v.* roo, haep.
heart *n.* hert.
heave *v.* bung, haeve, fire.

heed *v.* leet.
heifer *n.* quey, queyo.
held *v.p.p.* hadden.
Hello! *exclam.* Aye aye. Yaase min.
hen harrier *n.* catabellie.
hiccup *v.* hix. *n.* hippuck.
hillock *n.* howe, knowe.
hindmost *adj.* hinmost, himlest, himnest.
hip *n.* hench.
hit *v.* lunder, nap, pelter.
hoarse *adj.* krome.
hobble *v.* hirple.
hobnail boots *n.* tacketie buits.
hoe *n. & v.* howe.
hold *v. & n.* had, howld.
home *n.* hame, heem, hom.
hook *n.* huik, cruik.
hope *v.* hoop, hop.
hopscotch *n.* hipple-scotch.

hornless *adj.* cowed.
horse-fly *n.* cleg, bluidie-sooker.
hot *adj.* haet.
hot-tempered *adj.* bissie, birsable.
hour *n.* oor.
house *n.* hoose. **housework** hoosewark.
how *adv.* hoo.
howl *v.* gowl, yarm.
huge *adj.* wallie. **huge object** ark.
humming *adj.* nutheran.
humour *n.* (mood) cut, tune.
hundred *num.* hunder. **hundred-weight** hunder-weight.
hungry *adj.* fantan, tuim.
hurricane *n.* skreever.
hurry *n.* skitter. *v.* imse, pin, skint.
hurt *adj.* bruckit. *n.* bruckeen.
husk *n.* sid.
hysterical *adj.* ree, uim.

I

I *1st.pers.sing.* (+ am) Ah'm (+ will) Ah'll.
idiot *n.* nyaff.
ill *adj.* wersy.
ill-natured *adj.* ill-nettered.
immature *adj.* bairnlie, bairny.
improve *v.* come at.
incomer *n.* ferry-looper.
incompetent *adj.* gisless, handless.
inconvenience *v.* humbug.
indeed *exclam.* feth.
indolent *adj.* deuless.
indoors *adv.* in aboot.
inept *adj.* gisless, handless.
infect *v.* smit.
infectious *adj.* smitsome.

infer *v.* jalouse.
infuse *v.* mask.
injection *n.* jag.
injure *v.* mittle.
inquisitive *adj.* at-lukkan.
inside *adv.* inby, in-aboot.
insignificant *adj.* uddie.
insist *v.* thraep.
interfere *v.* middle.
intricate *adj.* footery.
invitation *n.* bid.
iris *n.* saegs.
island *n.* (small) holm.
it *pron.* hid. **itself** hidsael.
itch *v.* yuik.
itchy *adj.* yuikie.

J

jab *n.* jag.
jackdaw *n.* kae.
jacket *n.* jaiket.
jaundice *n.* gulsick.
jam-jar *n.* jeelie-jar.
jaws *n.* jaas, gams.
jelly *n.* jeelie.
jelly-fish *n.* klanker.

jersey *n.* gansey.
joke *n.* do, fun.
jolt *v.* childer, dilder.
journey *n.* (short) race.
jumble *v.* jummle.
jump *v.* loop, spret.
just right *adj.* the very dab.
jut out *v.* skoot.

K

keen on *adj.* mad for, yivverie.
kestrel *n.* moosie-haak, wind cuffer.
kick *v. & n.* keek.
kiln *n.* kill.
king *n.* keeng.
kitten *n.* ketleen.
kittiwake *n.* ritto, weeo.

knife *n.* gullie, tullie.
knock *n.* chap, ding, nap. *v.* chap. (into) dell.
knot *n.* raes.
know *v.* ken.
known *v.p.p.* kent.

L

lace *n.* (shoe) lacer.
lack *v. & n.* want.
landmark *n.* maithe.
lane *n.* closs, loan.
lap *n.* skurt.
lapwing *n.* teeo, teeick.
large object *n.* ark, clurt. **large number** *n.* dose, dreef, skreed.
lark *n.* sanlavro, laverock.
latch *n.* sneck.
late *adj.* backerlie.
laugh *v.* hix, cheeter, gelder. (loudly) golder.
law *n.* laa. **lawyer** lyer.
lazy *adj.* deuless. **lazy person** *n.* assie-pattle, fleep.

lean-to *n.* to-faa.
leather *n.* bend, bain.
left-handed *adj.* corrie-fisted.
leftovers *n.* aff-faas.
level *adj.* slite.
lightning *n.* weather blinks.
likely *adv.* liken.
limp *v.* hirple. *adj.* flamp.
linnet *n.* lintie.
lips *n.* (animals) mulls.
listless *adj.* domerless.
litter *n.* (animals) lyter.
little *adj.* peedie. *n.* aer, grain, shadie.
loan *n.* lend, laen.
lobster *n.* lapster.

loft *n.* laft.
long-tailed duck *n.* caloo.
look *v.* luk.
loose *v. & adj.* lowse.
lorry *n.* larry.
lose *v.* tyne. (one's way) will.
loss *n.* miss.

lot *n.* dose, jing-bang, lok.
loud *adj.* gowsterie, lood.
lukewarm *adj.* lew.
lull *n.* afftak, glett.
lump *n.* knorro, knurro.
lumpsucker *n.* steen-biter.
lurch *v. & n.* swander.

M

mad *adj.* gyte, ree, uim.
maggots *n.* arboo, maith.
make *v.* mak.
mallard *n.* wild-duck, stock-duck.
mallet *n.* maal.
manner *n.* atfers.
manure *n.* man'ure.
manx shearwater *n.* lyre.
many *adj.* haep o, dose o.
marble *n.* maalie.
mare's tail (bot.) *n.* trowie-spindle.
market *n.* market, mart.
marry *v.* maerry.
marsh marigold *n.* yellow gowan.
marshland *n.* loons.
mash *v.* chap.
master *n.* mester.
mastitis *n.* wade.
mat *n.* flakkie.
matted *adj.* wakkid.
matter *v. & n.* maetter.
mattress *n.* ma'trass, bedseck.
May *n.* Mey.
meadow *n.* meedow.
meadow-pipit *n.* hill-sparrow, teeteen.
meadow-sweet *n.* yule-girse.
meal *n.* mael. **meal-chest** girnal.
meddle *v.* middle. **meddlesome** *adj.* middlan.
meet *v.* fa in tow wi.

mention *v.* turn ower.
merganser *n.* herald duck.
mess *n.* aggle, haggis, gaggle, glergis, klatter, maes, plester, slaister, suck. *v.* (make a mess) aggle, haggle, gaggle.
messy *adj.* gushellie, slaisterie.
met *v.p.p.* mitten.
method *n.* atgyong.
mew *v.* nyow, yarm.
midden *n.* mideen.
midge *n.* mudjo.
minute *n.* meenit.
mischance *n.* misanter.
mischievous *adj.* ill-trickit, ill-veekit.
mist *n.* rug **misty** *adj.* ruggie, muggrofu.
mitten *n.* mogie.
mix up *v.* jummle.
moan *v. & n.* weh.
modern *adj.* modren.
moment *n.* blink, blinkie, glisk, peedie meenit.
monster *n.* Grullyan, Gyre.
moo *v.* bogle.
mood *n.* cut, gee, tune, stoond.
moody *adj.* stoondie.
moon *n.* muin.
moor-hen *n.* water-hen.
more *adv.* more, mair, better.

100

morsel *n.* skran.
mossy *adj.* foggie.
mostly *adv.* mostleens.
moth *n.* letter-flee.
mother *n.* mither.
mould *n.* niled, blue/green-niled.
  mouldy *adj.* niled, nilded.
moulting *adj.* in the kobos, in
  ossigar, in the pluck.
mound *n.* howe, knowe.
mouse-trap *n.* moose-fa.
mouth *n.* gab, gams, mooth.

move *v.* imse, mov, mudge oxter.
  (quickly) tramp, stoor. (house)
  flit.
movement *n.* sturt.
much *adj.* muckle.
mucus *n.* gurr.
mud *n.* gutter. **muddy** *adj.* gutterie.
mugwort *n.* grobie.
mumble *v.* mummle.
mussel *n.* yam, yug.
musty *adj.* foostie, moosened.
my *pron.* me.

N

nag *v.* sharg, yarg.
name *n.* name, neem.
nappy *n.* hippeen.
natural *adj.* netral.
naughty *adj.* ill-answeran.
nearby *adv.* aboot hands.
nearly *adv.* narleens.
neighbour *n.* neebor.
neither *adj.* nither.
nervous *adj.* skar, skart.
never *adv.* nivver.
news *n.* unkans.
New Year's Day *n.* Neuar-day.
nickname *n.* teu-neem.
nightdress *n.* goonie.
no *exclam.* na, naa, no.
nobody *pron* naebody, neebody.

noise *n.* dunder, golder. **make a
  noise** *v.* dunder, skirl, skolder,
  skroolt.
nonsense *n.* bulder, dirt, haivers.
  talk nonsense *v.* blether, haiver.
north *n.* nort.
Northern Lights *n.* Merry-dancers.
not *adv.* no. **not at all** *adv.* feentie-
  bit.
nothing *n.* feentie-thing, naetheen,
  notheen.
notion *n.* gee.
noughts and crosses *n.* trip-trap-
  truiskie, woggie-cattie-maggie.
now *adv.* noo. **nowadays** nooadays.
nuisance *n.* plester.

O

oats *n.* aets. **oatmeal** *n.* aetmael.
obey *v.* answer.
objectionable *adj.* come against.
obstinate *adj.* duggid.
obstreperous *adj.* obstrapalous.

obstruct *v.* backer.
occasional *adj.* anteran.
odd *adj.* neeborless.
off *prep.* aff.
offended *adj.* ap the spoot.

often *adv.* affens.
old *adj.* owld, aald.
old-fashioned *adj.* aald-farrant.
once *adv.* wance, eence.
one *num.* ane, een, wan.
open *v. & adj.* appen.
opposite *prep.* fornent.
orchis *n.* (purple) Adam, (early purple) deadman's liver, (pale mauve) Eve.
ordeal *n.* handleen.
other *adj.* ither. **(the)** t'ither.
our *pron.* wir, wur. **ours** *pron.* wirs.
ourselves *pron.* wirsaels.

out *adv.* oot. **out and about** *adv.* oot-aboot.
outbreak *n.* ootbrak. **outlook** ootluk.
outrageous *adj.* oot-be-telled.
over *prep.* ower, afore.
overturn *v.* whummle.
owl *n.* cattieface.
own *pron.* own, ain.
ox *n.* nout, owsin, stott. **oxen** oxies.
ox-eyed daisy *n.* gullan, karkit.
oyster catcher *n.* chalder, shalder, scottie, skeldro.

P

pack *v.* stap.
pace *n.* lick.
pail *n.* peel.
pain *n.* renyie.
palm (of hand) *n.* liv.
pampered child *n.* freck.
pant *v.* pech, whaese.
paper *n.* paeper.
particle *n.* stime.
particular *adj.* parteeclar.
party *n.* paerty, foy.
passage *n.* closs.
patched up *adj.* homeward bound.
pattern *n.* pattren.
pavement *n.* brigstones.
peace *n.* paece. **in peace** a-paece.
peat *n.* paet. **peat cutting tool** *n.* tusker.
peel *v.* fleester.
peep *v.* keek, teet.
peer *v.* glinder.
peevish *adj.* girnie, pleepie.
pell-mell *adv.* afore a face.
pen (for animals) *n.* buil.

people *n.* fock.
perch *n.* hallan, back.
periwinkle (shell) *n.* buckie.
persevere *v.* had at, stick in.
person *n.* buddie.
persuade *v.* tise.
perverse *adj.* stickid, thraan.
pester *v.* dore.
pet lamb *n.* caddie.
phosphorescence *n.* limro, mildroo.
pick *v.* plick.
picture *n.* picter.
pieces *n.* brucks, klatter.
pierce *v.* prog.
pig *n.* grice, soo.
pigeon *n.* doo.
pile *n.* roo, rookle.
pillow *n.* cod.
pimple *n.* plook, booick.
pin *n. & v.* preen.
pink *adj.* peenk.
pity *n.* peetie.
place *n.* piece.
plaice *n.* goldrick.

plant *v.* set.
plantain *n.* soldier.
plaster *v.* lagger.
plate *n.* ashet, plaet.
please *v.* plaese. **pleased** *adj.* blide, plaesed.
pleasant *adj.* lightsome.
pleasure *n.* wun.
plough *v.* ploo, brak oot.
   ploughshare *n.* sock.
plunder *v.* roop.
pocket *n.* pooch.
poison *n.* pooshon.
poke *n.* pock. *v.* pock, prog.
pony *n.* pownie.
poor *adj.* puir, trowie.
porpoise *n.* pallo.
porridge *n.* groal.
potato *n.* tattie. **potato masher** chappeen tree.
pot cleaner *n.* scratto.
pottery *n.* laem, leem.
pouch *n.* pooch.
pound *n.* (weight) pund.

pour *v.* poor, tuim.
pouting *adj.* mullsan, pootsan.
powder *n.* pooder.
praise *v.* rause.
prayers *n.* bonie-words.
precise *adj.* pernicketie.
preferable *adj.* morefare.
press together *v.* clam.
pretence *n.* makadeu.
pretend *v.* mak on, mak a deu, pit on.
pretty *adj.* bonnie.
prick *v.* dob, prog.
prickly *adj.* stobbie.
prim *adj.* perchink.
primrose *n.* mey flooer.
pudding *n.* puddeen.
puffin *n.* Tammie-norie.
pull *v.* pull, rive, rug, tweeg.
pullet *n.* arroo. (**-eggs**) arroo-eggs.
purple vetch *n.* moose-pea.
push *v.* shiv, shuit.
put *v.* pit *p.t.* pat, pot *p.p.* pitten. **put up with** *v.* thole.
putty *n.* pottie.

Q

quagmire *n.* quackoo.
quantity (small) *n.* aer, corn, grain, metteen, nert, puckle, sap, smithereen.
quantity (large) *n.* haep, hash, lock, mense.
quantity (of liquid) *n.* swash.
queasy *adj.* whamsy.

quench *v.* slock.
quick *adj.* queek.
quiet *adj.* (of a person) moothless.
   quiet! *exclam.* wheesht!
quilt *n.* twilt.
quit *v.* quite, white.
quiz *v.* whiss.

R

rabbit *n.* moppie.
rafters *n.* couples, backs.

rag *n.* pell, pelter. **ragged** *adj.* peltrie.

ragwort *n.* die-flooer, kemp.
rain *n.* dister, driv. *v.* mak weet, tuim.
ramshackle *adj.* unfaandoon, unfaansindrie.
rancid *adj.* ramse, tarf.
rat *n.* rattan.
rather *adv.* gey, kinda, rither.
ravine *n.* geo.
ravish *v.* rake on.
raw *adj.* raa.
razorbill *n.* coolter-neb, cooter-neb, sea-crow, skoot.
razor fish *n.* spoot.
reach *v.* raech, win tae.
really *adv.* ferly.
reason *n.* raison.
recently *adv.* short ago.
recollection *n.* mindeen.
red *adj.* red, reid.
red clover *n.* curlie-doddie.
redshank *n.* shankie.
redwing *n.* wind thrush.
reel *v.* stott *n.* purm.
related *adj.* sib.
relieve *v.* spell, speel.
reluctant (to) *adj.* aback o.
remember *v.* mind (on).
rennet *n.* yirneen(s).
repair *v.* trim.
restless *adj.* rampan.
restrain *v.* pit the haems on.
retribution *n.* back-comeen.

rheumatism *n.* rheumatics.
riddle *n.* godick.
ride *n.* hurl.
ridiculing *adj.* aff-takan.
ringed plover *n.* sanlo.
rip *n.* skirp.
rivet *v. & n.* clink.
roast *v.* rost.
rock *n.* klett, kungle.
rock pipit *n.* shore sparrow.
rod *n.* wand.
roe *n.* raan.
roll *v. & n.* row, rowl. **roll up** (sleeves) *v.* brett.
roof *n.* ruif.
rook/raven *n.* corbie.
rope *n.* raep.
rosin *n.* rosit.
rotten *adj.* feeskid.
rough *adj.* coorse, ramse, tarf.
rough treatment *n.* tuction.
round *adj.* roond.
row *v.* andoo.
rubbish *n.* bruck. **rubbish dump** bruckie roo.
ruin *n.* geldro, skatfa, vildro, windrift, winyo.
rump *n.* backside.
run *v.* pin, run. **run away** *v.* uptail.
rush *v.* rash.
rushes *n.* reshes.
rust *n.* roost.

S

sack *n.* seck.
sale *n.* roop.
same *adj.* sam. **same age** aboot ages, yammals.
sandgaper *n.* smerslin, soo shell.
sandpiper *n.* sandlark, steenie-picker.

sarcastic *adj.* aff-takan.
satisfactory *adj.* ower weel.
saucer *n.* sasser.
saunter *v.* andoo, dander, drilt.
saw *v.p.t.* saa.
saw *n.* saa.

scallop *n.* gimmer shell.
scare-crow *n.* tattie-bogle.
scarf *n.* gravit.
scatter *v.* skael.
scattering *n.* skaeliment.
scissors *n.* shears.
scold *v.* flyte (on).
scrape *v.* skuther.
scratch *v. & n.* cloor, scrat.
screech *v. & n.* skrek.
scythe *n.* sye.
seagull *n.* maa, whitemaa, cullyaw, skorie.
seal *n.* selkie.
seam *n.* saem.
sea mark *n.* maithe.
sea-pink *n.* arbie.
sea-scorpion *n.* sea-uikie.
seasick *adj.* whamsy.
seat *n.* saet. (in boat) thaft.
sea urchin *n.* scadman's heid.
seaweed *n.* droo, tang, tongles, ware, reidware.
see-saw *n.* happie-kindunkie.
seething *adj.* hudjan, (with anger) barman.
seize *v.* veeze.
select *v.* wael.
self *pron.* sael.
sense *n.* gy.
separate *v.* wael oot.
setback *n.* backereen.
sewer *n.* oddler, sester.
shabby *adj.* tuiltrie.
shag *n.* skarf, tapo.
shake *v.* dilder, dolder, pivver, shak, shoogle, weefle, shaft.
shaking *adj.* wafflie, weeflie.
shaky *adj.* shooglie.
shallow *adj.* showld.
she *pron.* sheu.
sheepmark *n.* aithken, uichen.

shelduck *n.* skeldro, slygoose, sheld fowl, skeeleen goose, ringer goose, scale duck.
shelf *n.* skelf.
shell *n.* buckie, grice, grottie-buckie, silver willie.
shellfish *n.* ebb maet.
shift *v.* imse, mudge, oxter.
shingle *n.* chingle.
shirt *n.* sark.
shiver *v.* grue.
shoal *n.* shald.
shoots *n.* breer.
shopping *n.* errands, messages.
shoulder *n.* shooder.
shout *v. & n.* golder.
show *v.* shaa.
shower *n.* dister, shooer. **showery** *adj.* blashie.
shrew *n.* sheermoose.
shrunk *adj.* clinkit, wakkid.
shut *v.* clam.
Shut up! *exclam.* Stoop! Stow!
shy *adj.* blate.
sick *adj.* seek, peelie-wallie.
sicken *v.* scunner.
sickle *n.* huik, hyuk.
sickly *adj.* dowie, trowie. (child) amis ting o bairn.
side by side *adv.* breid-band, cheek for chow.
sideways *adv.* sideleens, sidieweys.
sieve *n.* sye.
silly *adj.* tappie.
simple-minded *adj.* wantan.
since *prep.* fae.
singe *v.* swee.
sip *v.* sibble.
skate (fish) *n.* thornie-skate, torno.
skim *v.* (a stone over water) skeet.
skin *v.* fleep.

skua *n.* (Arctic) scootie-allan, (Great) bonxie.
skylark *n.* sanlavro.
slap *n.* lugget.
slash *v.* rit.
slice *n.* shaef.
slide *v.* skite.
slip knot *n.* runnan raes.
slobber *v.* slerp.
slope *n.* hing.
slovenly *adj.* brucksy.
sly *adj.* fly, sleekid.
smack *n.* skelp. *v.* pay, skelp.
small *adj.* peedie, peerie, sma, udmal.
smart *v.* swee.
smashed *adj.* mullie-fustered.
smear *v.* kline, lagger.
smell *n.* guff, reek, uind.
smelly *adj.* guffie, guffan, uinie.
smirk *v.* smikker.
smithereens *n.* mummie, shellmaleens, smook.
smithy *n.* smiddie.
smoke *v. & n.* reek, smok.
smooth *adj.* slite.
snag *n.* wifflo.
snatch *v.* click, glab, glam, wheek, whup.
snigger *v.* neester.
snipe *n.* snippo, horse-gock, heather-bleater, mire-snipe.
snorting *adj.* snushan.
snow *v.* smook, sna.
snow bunting *n.* snawie fowl.
snowdrift *n.* fann.
snowstorm *n.* blindroo, moor.
soak *v.* drook. soaked *adj.* bucksed, drookled, sabbid, sirpan, sypan.
sold *v.p.t.* selt.
solder *n.* sowder.
somehow *adv.* somewey.

somewhat *adv.* kinda, kindo.
somewhere *adv.* somepiece, somewey.
soot *n.* ime, seut.
sorrel *n.* soorick.
sorry *adj.* vexed.
sound *n.* soond.
sour *adj.* sharp, shilpit, soor.
south *n.* sooth.
souvenir *n.* faireen.
sow *n.* soo.
sow *v.* saa.
sparing *adj.* jimp, nippit.
sparkling *adj.* tullimentan.
sparrow *n.* sprug.
speak *v.* spaek.
speed *n.* lick, pin, redd.
spider *n.* ettercap, kirstie-kringlick, speeder.
spill *v.* lipper.
spin *v.* birl, birr, dirl, pirl.
spindly-legged *adj.* trindlie-leggit.
spoiled (child) *adj.* freckid.
spoke *n.* spoag.
spongy *adj.* foggie, fozie.
spoon *n.* spuin.
spout *n.* spoot, stroop.
spread *v.* clart, kline.
Spring *n.* Voar.
sprout *v.* breer, sproot.
squat *v.* sit on the hookers.
squeak *v.* weesk, weester. *n.* weesk.
squeeze *v.* briz.
squint *adj.* agee, glyed, skaoowaoo. squint-eyed glyed.
squirt *v.* skeet.
stab *v.* dob, prog.
stack *n.* cole, diss, skroo.
stagger *v.* stott, swander.
stall *n.* staa.
stallion *n.* staig.
stare *v.* gan, stime.

106

starling *n.* stiggie, stirleen, strill.
stars (to see) *v.* tae see kringlos.
start *v.* stert, tak tae.
stave (barrel) *n.* scow.
stay *v.* bide.
steal *v.* stael, roop.
stern *n.* starn.
stick *v.* clag. **sticky** *adj.* claggie.
stiff *adj.* breeksed.
still *adv.* a-paece.
sting *v.* swee.
stingy *adj.* near-begaan.
stink *n.* goo, guff, uin(d).
stir *v.* steer.
stirk *n.* strick.
stomach *n.* puggie.
stolen *v.p.p.* stelt.
stone *n.* stane, steen, ston.
stool *n.* creepie.
stop *v.* quite.
stormy-petrel *n.* alamootie, storm-finch.
straight *adj.* stryte.
strain *v.* sye. (oneself) breekse, spring.
strainer *n.* syer.
strange *adj.* unkan. **stranger** *n.* unkan buddy.
straw *n.* straa, strae. (bundle of) windleen.
stream *n.* burn.
strength *n.* feck.
stretch *v.* raek, rex, straek, straetch.

stride *n.* spang.
strike *v.* clipe, dunt, lunder, strick.
stripe *n.* strip. **striped** *adj.* strippid.
stroke *v.* straek.
stroll *v.* andoo, dander *n.* dander.
stumpy *adj.* puiltie.
stupid *adj.* gisless.
sturdy *adj.* vikkened.
substantial *adj.* wallie.
such *adj.* sic, seek.
suck *v. & n.* sook.
suffice *v.* dae the turn.
sugar *n.* shugger.
sulk *v.* poots, tak the poots, be in the dorts.
sulky *adj.* dortie, pootsie, pootsan.
sultry *adj.* muifie.
sunk *v.p.p.* sucken.
sun-spurge *n.* warite-girse.
supple *adj.* soople, swack.
suspect *v.* jalouse.
suspense *n.* tig-tag.
swallow *v.* gulup, klunk doon, quark.
swarm *v.* quack, skrullyie, skry. *n.* skrullyie, skry.
swell *v. & n.* swaal.
swig *n.* took.
swim *v.* sweem.
swindle *v. & n.* swick.
swindler *n.* swick.
swing *v.* weengle.
swoon *n.* dwam.
systematically *adv.* in a face.

T

table *n.* teeble.
tack *n.* (of boat) taek.
tackle *v.* set face tae.
take *v.* tak. **take care** *v.* caa canny.

talk *v.* spaek, (persistently) yap. **talk nonsense** *v.* blether, haiver.
talkative *adj.* gowsterie.
tangle *v.* raffle. *n.* fankle, frapp, raffle.

tap *n.* krans. *v.* pick.
tarpaulin *n.* tarpalyin.
tattered *adj.* fyoltrie.
tawny *adj.* tanny.
tear *v.* rive. *n.* skirp.
tedious *adj.* langsam, langersom.
telling off *n.* face-washeen, hod.
tell-tale *n.* clash-pie, clipe, tell-pie.
tell tales *v.* clipe.
temper (in a) *n.* dander (up).
temperamental *adj.* whiddie.
temporary mend *n.* by-pit.
tepid *adj.* lew.
tern *n.* pickie, ritto.
terribly *adv.* horrible, horrid.
than *prep.* as.
that *pron.* yin. *conj.* at
themselves *pron.* thirsaels.
then *adv.* than, then.
these *pron.* this.
thin out *v.* single.
thingummybob *n.* hoodjikapiv.
thistle *n.* tistle.
those *pron.* that wans, them.
thought *v.p.t.* thowt.
thousand *num.* thoosand.
thrashing *n.* boofleen.
threaten *v.* offer.
thrift (bot.) *n.* arbie.
throat *n.* craig, hass, thrapple.
throb *v.* tift.
throw *v.* ball, bung, fire, haeve, wap. (down) clash.
thud *n.* dad, dunt, tuink.
thumb *n.* toom.
thump *n.* drivas, dunk, tuink.
thwart *n.* thaft.
tickle *v.* kittle. tickly *adj.* kittlie.
tide race *n.* roost, rost.
tidy *v.* redd ap.
tight *adj.* thight.
tingle *v.* mirr.

tinker *n.* tinkler.
tin mug *n.* jeck.
tiny *adj.* peedie.
tip up *v.* coup, coop, cup.
tired *adj.* puggled, wabbit.
to *prep.* tae.
toad *n.* huppo, paddo.
today *adv.* the day.
toe *n.* tae.
told *v.p.t.* telled, tellt.
tom cat *n.* gibbie.
tomorrow *adv.* the morn. tomorrow night the morn's night. tomorrow morning the morn's morning.
tongs *n.* teengs.
tonight *adv.* the night.
too *adv.* teu.
took *v.p.t.* tuk, tuik.
tooth *n.* teeth, (molar) yackle.
toothache *n.* teethache, tuithache, worm.
top *n.* tap.
torch *n.* plicko, spunkie.
tossing *n.* heyse.
totter *v.* tilter.
tottering *adj.* ricklie, shooglie, tilterie, unfaandoon.
towel *n.* tooel.
tower *n.* tooer.
town *n.* toon.
trail behind *v.* drail.
trick *v.* gock. trickery *n.* jookerie-packerie.
trodden down *adj.* pattled.
troll *n.* trow.
trousers *n.* breeks.
trout *n.* troot.
tug *v.* yig, yirg.
turf *n.* divot, fail.
turn *v.* tirl, coop, wap.
turnip *n.* neep.
turnstone *n.* staneputter.

twelve *num.* twal.
twilight *n.* grimleens.
twist *v.* hink, kringle, nick, thraa, waffle. *n.* rink, snirl, snuid, fankle, kick.

twisted *adj.* skaoowaoo, in a fankle.
twite *n.* heather lintie.
two *num.* twa.

U

udder *n.* urrie, yurrie.
ugh! *exclam.* Gad! Gid-gad!
uncultivated land *n.* brecks.
undernourished *adj.* ill-triven.
unknown *adj.* unkan.
unlucky *adj.* ill-luckid.
unpredictable *adj.* gluffy.
unstable *adj.* weenklie.
unsteady *adj.* cocklie, shooglie, fyoltrie.

untidiness *n.* uivigar. **untidy** *adj.* brucksy, ravsie, tagsie.
unwell *adj.* aff the baet, trowie.
up *prep.* ap. **uppermost** uimest.
upon *prep.* apae, apin.
uproar *n.* rookery, wap.
upset *v.* coop, tirl.
us *pron.* is, his.
used up *adj.* at the hell-doors.
useless *adj.* deuless, fooshonless, handless.

V

vast *adj.* undeeman.
veer *v.* cast aboot.
very *adv.* aafil, ferfil, gey.
vest *n.* semmit.
vetch *n.* (meadow) fudsho. (purple) moose-pea.
veterinary surgeon *n.* veet.

vexed *adj.* grabbit, grypid.
vibrate *v.* pivver.
vicinity (in the) *adv.* aboot hands.
vole *n.* cutto, volder, voldro, volo.
volubility *n.* afflay.
vomit *n.* speweens.

W

wade *v.* wad.
waken *v.* wakken.
walk *v.* drilt, magse, pattle, steck, wak.
wall *n.* dyke, waa, (of turf) failie-dyke.
wander *v.* andoo, dander, stravaig.

washer *n.* roove.
waste away *v.* dwine.
water *n.* watter.
weak *adj.* wersy. **weak drink** *n.* blash, pleenk.
wedding *n.* waddeen.
weep *v.* greet.

weigh *v.* wey. **weight** *n.* wight.
well *n.* waal, wael. *adj.* weel.
went *v.p.t.* gaed, geed, gid.
wet *adj.* weet, (weather) blashie, hashie.
what *pron.* whit, whitan, whitna.
whatever *adv.* furtiver.
wheatear *n.* chackie, stinkie-buil, stone-chat.
wheel *v.* hurl. **wheelbarrow** *n.* hurlborrow.
wheeze *v.* whaese, wheer.
whelk *n.* wilk.
where *adv.* whar, wharaboots, wharpiece.
whetstone *n.* sharpeen stone.
whim *n.* stoond, whassigo.
whimbrel *n.* summer-whaap.
whine *v.* girn, weesk.
whirlpool *n.* swelkie.
whisper *v.* hark.
who *pron.* whar.
wick *n.* week.
wicked *adj.* weekid.

widow *n.* weedow-wife.
widower *n.* weedow-man.
wind *v.* wap, wup.
windy *adj.* gowsterie.
with *prep.* wae, wi. **without** *prep.* athoot.
woman *n.* wife. **women** *n.* weeman, weeman-fock.
wonder *v.* winder. **wonderful** *adj.* winderfil.
wood *n.* wid. **wooden** *adj.* widden.
wooden wedge *n.* dook.
woodlouse *n.* slatero.
wool *n.* oo. **woollen** *adj.* ooeen.
work *v.* wirk. *n.* wark.
worked *p.t.* wrowt.
worried *adj.* annoyed.
worse *adj.* waar, warse. **worst** warst.
would *v.p.t.* wad, wid.
wrapped up *adj.* happid.
wrasse *n.* bergel, bergilt, soofish.
wring *v.* thraa.
wrinkle *v.* ruckle.

Y

yarrow *n.* dog flooer, tea flooer.
yawn *v.* gant, yaan.
year *n.* 'ear.
yell *v. & n.* skrek.
yellow hammer *n.* yellow yarleen.
yes *exclam.* aye, ya, yaase, yass.

yolk *n.* reidba.
you *pron. sing.* thoo, thee. **yourself** theesael.
yowl *v.* nyarm.
yuck! *exclam.* Gad!